BUDDHIST REVIVAL IN INDIA

By the same author

The Buddha: Buddhist Civilisation in India and Ceylon
Buddha, Marx and God (second edition)
A History of Religion East and West
Karl Marx and Religion
Religious Change and the Secular State
Buddhism and the Mythology of Evil
Buddhism, Imperialism and War

BUDDHIST REVIVAL IN INDIA

Aspects of the sociology of Buddhism

Trevor Ling

Professor of Comparative Religion
University of Manchester

St. Martin's Press   New York

ISBN 0–312–10681–5

Library of Congress Cataloging in Publication Data

Ling, Trevor Oswald.
   Buddhist revival in India.

   Bibliography: p.
   Includes index.
   1. Buddhism—India—History.   2. Buddhism and
social problems—India.   I. Title.
BQ339.L56 1980   294.3′0954   79–20167
ISBN 0–312–10681–5

Contents

PART TWO
ANTI-BRAHMANISM AND NEO-BUDDHISM

Acknowledgements

I am grateful for permission to reproduce· some passages which have appeared elsewhere. Much of Chapter 4 appeared originally as a contribution to the volume *Pali and Buddhist Studies*, edited by A. K. Narain (New Delhi, 1979). Chapter 3 includes, in a revised form, some material from my contributions to the volumes *Man and His Salvation*, edited by J. R. Hinnells and E. Sharpe (1973), and *History and Society*, edited by Debiprasad Chattopadhyaya (Calcutta, 1978). Some passages in Chapter 7 are from my inaugural lecture at Leeds University, 'Max Weber in India', published in the *Leeds University Review*, May 1973. I should particularly like to mention the very generous help I have received from Mr Harish Chandra Gupta, Deputy Librarian of India's National Library, Calcutta, and to express my thanks to Mr Biswanath Chatterjee for his patient typing of my manuscript.

Calcutta, January 1979   T.L.

Part One

Buddhism and Brahmanism

1 Alienated Hindus

The Buddhist way for India's Untouchables

'India has not yet taken back the faith of her Emperor Ashoka.'
To Caroline Rhys Davids, writing these words from Manchester in 1910,[1] it might have seemed that the revival of Buddhism in India could not long be delayed, even although it had not yet begun. Nineteenth century European scholars had worked energetically and persistently at uncovering its historical origins. They had done so at a time when the Brahman view of ancient Indian history, 'in possession of the field when Europeans entered India, had been regarded so long with reverence,' commented T. W. Rhys Davids, that it seemed an impertinence to put forward any other.[2] The orthodox Hindu of India would have thought it better to leave well alone, he continued. 'Why resuscitate from the well-deserved oblivion in which, for so many centuries, they have happily lain, the pestilent views of these tiresome people [the Buddhists].'[3] But considerable progress in European knowledge of Indian Buddhist origins and history had been made, and by the beginning of the twentieth century it was sufficient to embolden writers such as the Rhys Davids to present a different and more honourable view of Buddhism than had been taken previously, a view based on archaeological and textual evidence which seriously challenged 'the Brahman theories of caste and history'.[4]

In Buddhism India had produced a system of thought which, European scholars were beginning to recognise, was in certain ways more congenial and certainly more intelligible to modern minds than that of the orthodox Brahmans, who had for so long been regarded as the sole representatives of Indian philosophy. By the beginning of the twentieth century, therefore, it seemed that not only to Europeans but to modern Indians, too, Buddhism

3

might make a new appeal, and be on the threshold of a revival.

Fifty years after Mrs Rhys Davids wrote her 'not yet' it began to seem as though India had at last recognisably begun to take back into her cultural life the Buddhist element which had for long been banished to a precarious existence in the mountainous fringes. Between 1951 and 1961 the Indian Census figures for Buddhists in the state of Maharashtra shot up from about two and a half thousand to more than three and three-quarter million. What had happened during that decade was the conversion of some of Maharashtra's former 'Untouchable' castes. The event can be variously interpreted. To some it may seem bizarre that the people of a modern state should resort to the adoption of an ancient religion as an effective means of remedying their social and economic deprivation. To others it may look initially like another case of a new religious sect arising out of a situation of social, economic and political frustration. By yet others it may be hailed as the dawn of a new era in which Buddhism in India is at last beginning to come to life again. Whatever view is eventually taken, whether one of these or some other, one must first consider the circumstances in which this growth began, and the nature of what has emerged.

The movement began publicly in 1956 when Dr Bhimrao Raji Ambedkar, himself of low-caste origin, announced his conversion to Buddhism, and recommended this course of action to the entire community of India's Scheduled Castes.[5] This policy is still being pursued by some of those who have succeeded him in the leadership of the 'neo-Buddhists', as he himself called them.[6]

However, not all the Scheduled Castes by any means, nor even the majority of them, have become or appear likely to become Buddhists. By 1971 the Scheduled Castes of India numbered altogether about sixty-six million. The minority of three million or so who became Buddhists, and are returned as such in the Census figures for 1971, are mainly from two caste groups found in Maharashtra state and the adjacent districts in surrounding states, and in Agra City in the state of Uttar Pradesh. The majority of their Scheduled Caste fellows are either seeking other remedies for their socially and economically deprived condition, or are still passively acquiescing in their centuries-old inherited inferiority. But this attitude is less common nowadays, and this may be an indirect result of Ambedkar's activities.

Some observers have regarded Ambedkar's policy as an entirely

4

inappropriate way of dealing with a complex social and economic problem. It is possible that his policy is to be interpreted as the expression of misplaced Buddhist piety; or perhaps as political miscalculation, the lessons of which must now be noted for the benefit of those who are seeking other remedies. This raises the question of the value of what may be called 'the Buddhist way for Untouchables'. In order to deal adequately with such issues it is necessary to consider the nature of the new Buddhist movement as it developed during the decade and a half subsequent to the great public conversion ceremonies of 1956, and to view the events of that period in the perspective of the preceding thirty years of Ambedkar's public activity, from about 1924 when—soon after his return to India from postgraduate social science and legal studies in New York and London—he founded the Society for the Benefit of the Excluded Classes.[7] Moreover, the essential background against which Ambedkar's neo-Buddhist movement has to be set is that of the Hindu social order as it existed (in a truncated form it is true, but still possessed of considerable strength) under British rule, and as it has persisted since. Some preliminary observations of a general nature concerning Hindu religion are necessary at this point.

The Hindu social order

That so large a section of India's Hindu population should have continued to suffer social oppression at the hands of their fellow Hindus is not a novel phenomenon in the annals of religion. Contrary to the views of idealists it is a fairly common type of occurrence. The brutal treatment of Bengali Muslims by their fellow Muslims of Pakistan; the social disabilities suffered by English Nonconformists in the nineteenth century at the hands of the Church of England; the attitude of Ceylon's high-caste Kandyan Buddhists towards their low-caste fellow Buddhists of the coastal plains: these are similar examples of a characteristic of established institutional religion which is too well known to be regarded as exceptional when it is found among Hindus.

However, there might seem to be a special inappropriateness about such oppression in this case, for Hinduism projects to the outside world an image which could be said to be composed in equal parts of *tolerance, spirituality* and *unity*. At the level of ideas,

5

these qualities are without doubt characteristic of Hinduism. Adherents and supporters of Hindu religion are tolerant not only of those who agree with them whatever their religion, but even also of many who do not. Moreover, Hindus do not normally criticise the conduct of the adherents of other religions unless it touches on some matter very crucial to them (such as the sacrifice of a cow by Muslims, or missionary work by Christians).

Tolerance is readily extended by Hindus at the metaphysical level. Observers often comment on the easy ideological pluralism of Hindu religion. In Hinduism, it is said, one may believe whatever one likes. More exactly, there is a great readiness to adopt a socially tolerant attitude to the expression of any variety or number of metaphysical theories so long as they are not in direct contradiction with some cardinal Brahmanical doctrine, such as that of the eternal existence of the soul and its continual transmigration through many lives until *mukti* or release is obtained. But Buddhists, who dissent from this belief in the eternal existence of the soul, are condemned in traditional Brahman terminology as *nastika*, or heretics. Thus, in theory, there is absolute tolerance, but in practice it is conditional. For no more than the adherents of any other religious ideology which claims to enshrine absolute and eternal truth can orthodox Hinduism's representatives afford to allow profane questionings of the uniquely sublime character of their system or of the necessity for absolute acceptance of certain 'eternally true' key doctrines.

As for *spirituality*, it is undeniable that Hinduism's exponents and promoters, at any rate, are preoccupied with this feature of their religion. This is most notably the case when they are addressing a Western audience or readership. The habit of contrasting Hindu 'spirituality' with Western 'materialism', a habit which began in the nineteenth century in response to British rule and its cultural consequences, has now become a firmly established feature of Hinduistic ideologies of all kinds. Indeed, for aristocratic members of the upper castes it may really seem that Hindus are largely indifferent to material concerns. It has to be remembered also, however, in order to keep a realistic perspective on this issue, that the upper castes, who are the main bearers and exponents of this notion of Hindu indifference to material interest, have, through the centuries, *as a class* maintained a generally privileged material and social condition. Those less fortunately placed in the social hierarchy may not find it possible to agree so easily

6

with the claim that Hindus (especially Hinduism's most ardent upholders) are indifferent to material interests. The vast majority of such potential dissenters are, however, largely inarticulate where such matters are concerned, and certainly where Western audiences are concerned. They have throughout the centuries been denied the right to education and the material benefits it conveyed (just as were serfs in feudal Europe and most of the proletariat in England up to the latter part of the nineteenth century), and they were very definitely not regarded as being in a position to express their views on the nature of Hindu religion, for they were by Hindu canons of law forbidden even to hear the sacred words of the Vedic scriptures. Thus, material interests can be said to be a matter of indifference to orthodox-caste Hindus—in theory; but historical and social evidence suggests something different in practice.

As far as unity is concerned this too is a great theoretical preoccupation. The concept of non-duality (*advaita*) is central to Hindu philosophical idealism. This is a sufficiently well-known form of metaphysics to need no elaboration here. The popular exposition of Hindu religious ideas in terms of Advaita Vedanta has been familiar to the West at least since the migration of Aldous Huxley and his associates to California in the 1930s. The preoccupation of Hindu metaphysics with the idea that non-duality characterises the ultimate nature of everything is rather curious, and possibly significant, in view of the dividedness and lack of cohesion which actually characterises Hindu society. The 'minorities' of India, as they are officially known, are not merely the Muslims, Sikhs, Christians, Buddhists and so on, for, as it has often been pointed out, everyone in India, including the Hindu, belongs to a minority group of some sort. Indeed it is more true of Hindus than of others, for the narrow limits within which social communication can occur within the caste system, the weak sense of social solidarity and the lack of social cohesion have been commented on by observers from the time of Al-Biruni, if not earlier. One does not condone imperialism by pointing out that it was not necessary for the British to 'divide and rule', as they were accused by Indian nationalists of having done. The divisions were already there in India, multiple and well-established. In the matter of unity, therefore, it seems once again that Hindu idealist theory stands in contrast to historical and social reality.

If, therefore, the conclusion is that Hinduism, in terms of its metaphysical theory is characterised by tolerance, spirituality and unity, but in terms of its social reality by ultimate intolerance, disguised material interest and pervasive disunity, it has to be added that in this respect it is not unique among institutional religions. In all such complex formations the degree of inconsistency between social reality and metaphysical ideal, and the significance of such inconsistency, constitute important and still insufficiently investigated problems in the sociology of religion.

Meanwhile, we may note that on the one hand Hindu metaphysical ideas and spirituality certainly make up a well known and much-advertised area in the study of religion. On the other hand, the Hindu social order, deriving its nature and structure from the classical prestige and privilege which was enjoyed by the Brahman class, and from the subsequent imitation of the Brahman's style by subordinate castes, a phenomenon which may be described broadly as Brahmanism, has received less attention. In this way an important dimension has been omitted from the study both of Hinduism and of Indian Buddhism. It is with Brahmanism in this sense that the present study will be concerned.

The growth of dissent

From the early years of the twentieth century an uneasy awareness of the contrast between metaphysical theory and social reality began to stir a number of Hindu reformers to attempt some correction. Thus, the cause of the low castes—the Untouchables—was taken up by Gandhi, who declared that his aim was the eradication of Untouchability from Hindu society. But he wished also to see caste institutions and the four-fold categories of caste, the *caturvarna*, preserved. It is not altogether clear that these two aims were compatible. Moreover, his advocacy of the idea of *Ramraj*—that is, society ruled by Rama, the Hindu god—was another indication of how 'reformed' the Hindu social order would have been if he had had his way.

Ambedkar was Gandhi's most serious rival as champion of the cause of the Untouchables. In fact, it was with some difficulty that Gandhi tried to make his claim to be a more credible representative of the Untouchables than this outstanding member of that community who by dint of his own and his father's extraordinary and pertinacious efforts had become equally as well-educated and professionally qualified as Gandhi, the caste Hindu. Ambedkar, moreover, was deeply involved in the day-to-day life of the Untouchable Mahar community in Bombay. It was essential for Gandhi to deny Ambedkar's credentials, however, for the latter's total rejection of the Hindu social order was entirely unacceptable to the interests Gandhi represented.

Towards the end of the thirty years of his intensely active life of struggle on behalf of the Untouchables Ambedkar decided, just before his death in 1956, to espouse Buddhism publicly. This, it seemed to him, offered the Untouchables, if they would follow him, the best hope of escape from the oppression they suffered as Hindus. In certain respects it was a brave decision, particularly as there was virtually no Buddhist community to speak of in existence in India at that time. It was also a curious and even, possibly, a rather rash decision, in view of the fact that Buddhists as a community had disappeared from almost all of India seven or eight centuries before, and had done so in circumstances which could still hold menacing possibilities for any attempt to re-establish Buddhism in India on a wide scale. In order to assess the cogency of Ambedkar's decision, and its implications for the Untouchables of India both now and in the future, it is proposed here, first to investigate the causes of Buddhism's disappearance from ancient India, and second to enquire whether the situation in modern India is now sufficiently different for Buddhism to stand a better chance of being re-established than it has had at any time during the past eight centuries. A further question to be investigated, and one which relates to the first two, is whether in any case Buddhism can, at the end of the twentieth century be regarded as offering *by itself* a viable alternative to those in particular who, placed as they are at the bottom of the Hindu ritual and social scale, increasingly find their situation intolerable. But it is not only for them but for others, from the educated middle classes, that the possibility of the restoration of Buddhism in India is a matter of urgent interest.

Apart from studies of the life and work of Dr Ambedkar,[8] three writers in particular—Fiske, Lynch and Zelliott—have contributed substantially to the study of the new Buddhist movement in India as it has developed since Ambedkar's death. Fiske has dealt with it primarily as an example of a *religious* movement arising out of conditions of social deprivation, while Lynch and Zelliott in their accounts have dealt mainly with the political aspects of the movement, in Agra City and Maharashtra respectively.[9] My purpose here is to put Ambedkar's work and the neo-

Buddhist movement he inaugurated into the context of Buddhism in the world of the twentieth century. In doing so I hope to show some implications which are relevant to the sociology of religion, and particularly for the working out of a typology of Buddhist formations.

2 Buddhist popularity in India

What became of Indian Buddhism?

There is something of a mystery about Buddhism in India. An Indian colleague once put it to me this way: 'Buddhism could never have been really popular; if it had been really popular, it could never have completely died out.' To this well-hedged proposition I was prepared to assent, but for one possibility it seemed he had left out: 'Unless, of course, it was murdered.'

It is, in fact, now being claimed that Buddhism has in India recently begun to respond to attempts to revive it. But if it died a natural death, as many have claimed that it did, then these recent efforts to revive it, even inspired as they are by admiration for Buddhism's socially equalitarian character, might appear to be in the same class as an attempt at the artificial respiration of a corpse.

Analogies of this sort are useful in provoking thought, but cannot be pressed too far, and cannot be a good guide to the nature of social realities such as the one we are concerned with. What is required is a careful exploration of historical and social issues, and comparison with other relevant cases. That is the kind of enterprise which is envisaged here. Alongside the case of Buddhism in India we shall consider that of Burma.

Perhaps no really popular religion ever does completely die out. This still does not disperse the mystery about Indian Buddhism. One is left to choose between a number of puzzling possibilities. For example, the implication may be that Buddhism in India was never really *popular*. But was it not? This is at least a debatable issue. Another implication is that it was popular, and that it did not die out but changed, assumed another form or went underground like an Indian river in the dry season, still flowing a few feet below the sandy surface of the sun-bleached river bed. Dig a

11

well only ten feet deep in that dried-up channel—as I have seen it done in Bihar—and there below is the water, still flowing slowly, available for irrigating the fields around.

Which of these two main possibilities provides the more probable explanation it is part of our purpose here to investigate. The first of the two—that Buddhism was never really popular in India—will be the main concern of this chapter.

As to the second—that Buddhism never really died—there are three ways of envisaging this possibility:

1. Buddhism may have persisted in the popular culture but in other forms;
2. it may have gone underground and still be feeding the roots of Indian culture; or
3. it may have retreated to the fringes of India, like grass worn away by excessively heavy traffic, now tenaciously maintaining itself at the edges, ready at the arrival of changed conditions to spread back again.

For it is at the fringes of India as a culture area that Buddhists are still to be found, in the north-west, the north-east and the extreme south. Whether Buddhism maintains itself in those places tenaciously or merely precariously is, however, open to question. The question will in fact be raised in the fourth chapter, when a survey is made of the present extent of the Buddhist population of India. Of the other two ways of envisaging Buddhism's persistence, that is, 1. and 2., the first can be dealt with now; the second of them will be raised again in connection with the so-called neo-Buddhism of the twentieth century.

The theory that Buddhism *was* popular, and that it did *not* die out but simply changed and persists in some other form, requires, if it is to be acceptable, that it persists in India today in some form which is as popular and as widespread as when (in this theory) it openly existed in Buddhist form. For this to be the case, something more than was envisaged in Hariprasad Sastri's theory is required. Sastri put forward the idea that the village cult of Bengal, which goes by the name of the Dharmaraja cult, is the form in which Buddhist religion survives in that region of India where it had persisted longest. This theory is, in any event, now generally regarded as untenable. The village worship of

12

Dharmaraja has other roots: it may well be a fertility cult; it may be totemistic; it may, on good evidence, be regarded as a relic of sun-worship. From its characteristic features these all are possibilities, but it is fairly certainly *not* a vestigial form of the Buddha-Dharma.[1]

Such survival would in any case have been tantamount to no survival. Any respectable 'survival theory' requires that there exists in India some widespread, popular movement whose historical origins are at least approximately contemporaneous with the demise of institutional Buddhism. It is difficult to find a candidate with these qualifications. One might propose some who come somewhere near it, but none which fully satisfies the requirements in the way that would be necessary for this to be a convincing explanation of what became of Buddhist religion.

The implications of my Indian colleague's assertion, in so far as they have not already been dealt with summarily, will therefore provide the starting point for a general introductory survey of Indian Buddhist history in its later phases. There are also the implications of the suggestion about murder to be explored. Perhaps murder is too strong, too emotive a word in this case, however. Perhaps one should consider the idea that, if not murdered, Buddhism was vandalised, like a field of fine, flourishing mango trees viciously cut down by the jealous owner of a neighbouring coconut grove. And if we speak not of mangos but of Bo-trees being cut down then we are, to mix metaphors, getting rather near the bone. The Bodhi or Bo-tree is to the Buddhist the symbol of the Buddha's enlightenment, and in India it has certainly not been unknown for hostile non-Buddhist kings to cut down such trees, literally.

This kind of explanation—that Buddhism in India was, so to speak, vandalised—will be explored also in the first part of the book, and then will be considered in connection with the idea that Buddhism has not died but has only retreated to the fringes of India. To change the metaphor, we shall be enquiring about the possibility of an area now denuded of mango (or Bodhi) trees being rehabilitated—in other words, about the prospect of the trees being replanted there some day, for Bodhi trees still grow in the Buddhist borders of India. This will be the main concern of the second and third parts of this book.

13

Varieties of Buddhist culture

First, then, to be considered, is the question whether Buddhism was ever really *popular* in India, or whether, on the other hand, it was never anything more than a genteel, intellectual doctrine which, like a delicate potted plant, rested on the surface but never took root in the underlying culture. In order to answer this question satisfactorily it will be necessary to concern ourselves rather less with Buddhism and rather more with Buddhists; in particular, with the Buddhists of India and of Burma, past and present.

The reason for making this kind of emphasis is, briefly, as follows. The word 'Buddhism' can mean, first, a set of doctrines: in that case one has to acknowledge that a number of such related ideologies exist or have existed in various parts of Asia at various periods of time, each of which differs in some degree from the others. 'Buddhism' can mean also a type of culture. Here again, a number of varieties exist: South Indian Buddhism, Bengal Buddhism, Sinhalese Buddhism, Burmese Buddhism, Thai, Cambodian, Tibetan, Japanese and so on. Each of these is the product of interaction between the cultural form in which Buddhism originally reached the region concerned and the indigenous culture of that region. Whether these all have equal validity as 'Buddhist' cultures, or whether there is a paradigm Buddhism with which all should be compared is one of the questions to be raised in the course of this study. In any case, there is no international Buddhist hierarchy which can decide what is true Buddhism, or attempt to operate control; every sovereign country into which Buddhist ideas find their way can if it wishes attempt to mould the form which Buddhist culture takes in that country, as has been the case very clearly, for example, in Thailand. However, cultural change is not always controllable by political means, and in the last resort Buddhist cultural patterns will be shaped by a variety of factors, not the least important of which is likely to be the relative strength of the Buddhist presence, or, to put it another way, the nature and social composition of that part of the population who call themselves Buddhists. Because it is the purpose of this study to open up some of these questions, its main concern will be with Buddhists themselves, in India and Burma, rather than with the canonical orthodoxy to which they variously give or have given formal assent.

From any total set of received doctrines some are selected and given practical prominence while others are for practical purposes ignored. This kind of pragmatic selection from the range of doctrines available is not unknown in other 'world' religions, although in some it is made more difficult by ecclesiastical or similar control in the interests of orthodoxy. The extent of such control depends to some extent on the degree of political power enjoyed by the guardians of orthodoxy, or on their social status, or charismatic power, or their possession of some other means of exercising control or operating sanctions. Even so, the actualities of religious practice, and even of belief, may still not coincide with the canons of orthodoxy.

Such discrepancies can, of course, be explained in various ways, even explained away, by apologists of the tradition concerned. The type of explanation favoured here is simply that human beings are not pure spirits or pure intelligences, and they therefore cannot live by ideas alone. Humans are material beings with material needs: food, shelter and clothing, however basic and however minimal. These physical needs will inevitably to some extent condition human courses of action. They may also diminish the likelihood of absolute adherence to, in this case, prescribed Buddhist norms. This is not a materialistic account of the human situation but a realistic one; we are all so familiar with its reality that it would hardly be necessary to mention such matters were it not for the simple equation which is sometimes assumed to exist between religious ideals and actualities. In the past much has been written about Buddhist norms and ideals largely on the evidence of the canonical texts, but comparatively little, until recently, about the actualities of belief and practice among people who are called Buddhists, for it was generally assumed that they behaved and believed in the ways outlined in the texts. All but the largest and most unmistakable cultural variations were supposed not to exist.

Max Weber's study of Buddhism

In his insistence that genuine understanding of the nature and function of religion requires a study of what people *really* believe and practise, as distinct from what they are supposed to believe and practise, Max Weber pioneered the modern sociological

15

study of religion. He also coined the term *Religionssoziologie* for the social analytical approach to world religions and was in that sense the founder of the comparative sociology of religion.[2]

What Buddhists were supposed to believe, compared with what the evidence available may suggest they did believe, what lines of action they followed in various different historical and social situations, what were the accompanying social, political and material pressures to which they were subjected, and what came out of such complex interaction: these are the questions to which answers are needed, not only in the case of Buddhists but in those of other religious ideologies also. Here we shall be concerned with some of these issues in so far as they relate to the Buddhists of India and Burma. Broadly, therefore, the approach may be said to be Weberian.

It was Weber who recognised the need to distinguish between different *types* of Buddhism. He perceived that there was an initial stage when the teaching of the Buddha was transmitted within a small circle of world-renouncing, meditation-practising disciples who recognised that salvation was only for the few. This 'ancient Buddhism', as Weber called it,[3] was later succeeded by a more popular cult of devotion; this 'transformation of ancient Buddhism', whereby it became a mass religion, occurred, it is generally agreed, somewhere within the Ashokan period.

Ashoka, who was the ruler of an empire greater in size than any which had existed in India previously and which until the modern period was equalled again only by that of the Mughals, did for Buddhist religion, in one sense at least,[4] what the Roman emperor Constantine did for the Christian religion: he put it on the map. The practice of colouring large areas of world maps to show what in those areas is the 'dominant' religion is in essence a legacy of the Ashokan and Constantinian transformations into imperial religions of what had formerly been sects. Once this had been done, adherence to these religions became less a matter of choice or conversion or experience, and more one of social and cultural conformity. Until well into the modern period the inhabitants of European countries were assumed to be Christians, and the inhabitants of certain Asian countries such as Burma and Thailand were assumed to be Buddhists, in the senses which orthodoxy gives those names. It was this kind of assumption that Weber challenged. He insisted on the importance of correct characterisation. Not only was 'Christian' so vague and general a term as to be useless in any precise analysis, but even 'Protestant' had to be broken down until the effective unities of belief and attitude and ethical practice were reached. Proper distinctions could then be made between these collectivities which had now been identified.

Until recently, Western accounts of Buddhist religious organisation concentrated on the community of monks, the Sangha, and tended to regard it as fairly simple in structure—for example, the Sangha in Burma was treated in the literature of the subject as though it were a unitary body to which consistency of attitude and belief could be attributed. One of the major contributions to the sociology of Buddhist religion made by Michael Mendelson on the basis of his fieldwork in central Burma has been the serious doubt which he has thrown on the notion that it is possible to make any valid comprehensive general statements about 'the Sangha' in Burma, or that it is simply Theravadin in its norms and values.[5]

It is doubtful whether the Sangha was ever a single entity having an entirely homogenous character. It has usually existed as an assemblage of fairly independent congregations of monks, except as in Thailand in the modern period, where it has been part of the deliberate policy of the rulers of the country to impose a single hierarchical structure upon it. It was in association with the rule of the Indian emperor Ashoka that something akin to this process began, when the attempt was made to subject contrasting or conflicting schools of thought to imperial pressure. The result was that a large part of the total number of monastic groups took general shape as a community, acknowledging the authority of a defined corpus of Buddhist texts, and not only supported but also protected by the political ruler. As Weber pointed out, the transformation thus occurred of what had formerly been a congeries of small groups—all holding with varying degrees of emphasis an esoteric, world-renouncing and soul-denying philosophy—into a popular cult with permanent congregations of laymen, professionals who accepted responsibility for manning the cult and instructing the laymen, and agreement that what was now to be regarded as the authentic tradition, embodied in the Pali language, was: (1) the Buddha's discourses, (2) the code of discipline for the order of monks, and (3) the sets of lists and tables in which the doctrine was analysed and summarised. These three parts of the tradition were known respectively as the *Sutta*, the *Vinaya* and the *Abhidhamma*. Together they form the Pali canon of scripture,

17

and these have been adopted as the foundation documents of Theravada Buddhism.

How much of the contents of the Pali canon can be attributed to the historical Gautama Buddha may be questioned. What does appear to be more certain is that the system of beliefs and practice reflected in these texts is the Buddhism which flourished in India in the Ashokan period. The principal point of distinction from other philosophies and ideologies of the time was the denial of any permanent, unchanging individual self or soul, and the insistence that it was this false notion which lay at the root of human ills. Connected with this analysis of the human condition was another feature, unique—in the first instance at any rate—to Buddhism, and that was the concept of a community called the Sangha. The name Sangha had formerly been applied to the old tribal republics which were in the Buddha's day fast disappearing in the Gangetic plain before the onward march of the great monarchies, Koshala and Magadha. In one of these tribal republics, that of the Shakyas, Gautama had been brought up; his father was one of the leading citizens of this small state which was, in political structure, somewhere in between a tribal republic and a monarchy. Closely associated with the growth of towns, the diversification of the economy and the spread of monarchical government was the emergence of a marked spirit of individualism. It is significant that the vast majority of the discourses of the Buddha in the Pali canon are represented as having been delivered in one or other of the two great royal cities of the time, Shravasti and Rajagriha. In the face of the growing malaise or *anomie* of the time, associated as it was with the growth of individualism, the Buddhist solution was the rejection of the notion of the individual self; not merely in theory, however, but in practice. In the life of the new Sangha human existence was to be reconstituted and the weakness which had undermined the old tribal Sanghas—or assemblies of elders—and led to their downfall, namely the growth of selfish dissension and personal ambition, was to be eliminated. In early Buddhism the primary arena of salvation appears therefore to have been, normally at any rate (exceptions can be found), the common life of the Sangha; whether or not this was to be formally organised in a hierarchical manner, the fact remains that the idea of a *universal* Sangha appears to have been present from an early stage.

Buddhists and the political order

There are hints in some early Buddhist texts of an ambiguous attitude towards secular rulers. There are suggestions that from a Buddhist point of view a king is by the nature of his duties a man not to be envied and one who can live a meritorious life only with great difficulty. On the other hand there is much in the early tradition which appears to admit the necessity of rulers, human nature and society being what it is. But it is also strongly emphasised that the ruler should be one who acts not arbitrarily or tyrannically but wisely and with justice.

The ideal, therefore, described in the Buddhist texts is the Cakravartin, the world-ruler, and it was to this ideal that actual rulers such as Asoka of India and Devanampiya Tissa of Sri Lanka sought to approximate themselves and their policies. The restraining of the violent elements in society, the discouragement of crime by the alleviation of poverty, the provision of the material necessities to enable the citizens of the state to pursue the Buddhist life unhindered—these were the aims, and to some extent the achievements, of Buddhist rulers of the sort who have just been mentioned.

In such situations a triangular relationship of a close and intimate kind developed between the Sangha, the ruler and the people. The Sangha advised the ruler, guided him in the Dharma and supported him in his administration of the state. In return he provided protection for the Sangha and engaged in public works of stupa and monastery building and in ensuring optimum conditions for their pursuit of the Buddhist way. Of this the Sangha are, so to speak, the vanguard; in the classical type of Buddhism they are expected to be the growing points or 'cells' of restructured consciousness and a restructured society.

Between the ruler and people, according to this teaching, there is expected to be a reciprocal relationship of respect and support; without an efficient ruler society reverts to the law of the fishes, where large devour small; on the other hand, without loyalty from the people, and due observance of laws which are made for the benefit of all, the ruler cannot function efficiently or humanely and must necessarily become either a tyrant or a puppet. Between the Sangha and the people there is a similar reciprocal relationship of respect and support. The nature of that relationship will be described in the next chapter.

This pattern goes beyond what is envisaged in the *Suttas*. True, the discourses of the Buddha are by no means 'other-worldly'. As the son of one upon whom was laid responsibility for the ordering of the public affairs of the Shakya state, he himself was the friend and adviser of the kings of his day, such as Bimbisara and Pasenadi. A number of the *Jataka* stories contain descriptions of the ideal king. In the *Kutadanta*, the *Maha-Sudassana*, the *Cakkavatti Sihananda Suttas* and elsewhere, a good deal is said concerning the function of the righteous king; there is a clear implication that such righteous rule is desirable for providing optimum conditions for the Buddhist cure for the human malaise. So when Asoka turned in revulsion from the Brahmanically dominated statecraft exemplified in the famous *Arthasastra* it was to another ideal that he turned—to the Buddha-Dharma. It may have been during Ashoka's reign that the development in the relations of king and monks began which eventually linked Sangha, king and people in the threefold structure just described. This pattern is certainly presupposed in the events connected with the establishment of the Buddhist state in Sri Lanka under Devanampiya Tissa by emissaries from Ashoka.

As far as the lay people were concerned the emergence of the Ashokan pattern meant also the development of a code of lay morality. There were the five basic precepts: namely, abstinence from any violence to living beings, from stealing, from sexual immorality, from falsehood and from the use of alcohol and other drugs. In addition to these five, a number of other moral and social obligations came to be recognised and codified. They are described in the Sigalovada Sutta, allegedly a discourse of the Buddha, found in the Pali canon. The Sutta contains explicit teaching on social duties towards one's parents, teachers, wife and children, friends, workpeople and religious mentors. This Sutta is known also as the Gihivinaya—that is, the householder's code of discipline, a title which emphasises the fact that 'Buddhists' were now clearly recognised as consisting of laymen as well as monks.

Not only was a just and wise ruler and protector desirable from the Pali Buddhist point of view, but Buddhism also was desirable from the ruler's point of view, for it was a very useful adjunct to good government. This was so in South-East Asia as well as in India. As a religion Buddhism had the virtue of being non-priestly and therefore more acceptable to a ruling class who in India were themselves sometimes rivals of the Brahman priests. Moreover,

Buddhist monks were much cheaper to support than the Brahmans, who charged high fees. The social ethic which Buddhism provided meant that the ordinary people were likely to develop habits of peaceableness, generosity and sobriety. These are three of the more obvious advantages which Buddhism possessed in the eyes of Asian rulers, both in ancient and in medieval times.

The consequence of the adoption of Buddhism by political rulers raises an issue of some importance for the understanding of the development of Buddhist culture. A highly urbane, abstract analysis of the nature of the world, coupled with a practice of meditation based upon this analysis of a kind which is more likely to have an appeal to sophisticated townsmen, came in this way, through having been adopted *by kings* on account of its socially useful features, to be associated in practice with the folk-customs and ideas of a predominantly rural culture, where it had the effect of infusing these folk-cultures with Buddhist values to some extent, varying from place to place, and according to local circumstances.

What is not always recognised is that the Pali texts also demonstrate the existence of what may be called an open frontier between the Dharma and the local cults. The very fertile relationship which has existed between these two was misunderstood by early Western observers of Buddhism in Ceylon and South-East Asia. The notion grew up that Burmese Buddhism, for example, was 'really' only a thin layer of Pali Buddhism spread as a veneer over a vast mass of primitive 'animism' and other pagan practices.[6]

The idea of layers and veneers is not very helpful in cultural analysis. More appropriately it can be said that once such a Buddhist populace had become a feature of the scene, consisting as it did mainly of village people, it was natural that considerable popularising of the Buddhist cult took place. It is well known that this process was strongly aided by developments in Buddhist thought in India which occurred from about the first century BC, and which resulted in the emergence of a new type of Buddhism known as 'Mahayana', itself a terminology taken from popular speech. This means the great (*Maha*) vehicle or carriage (*Yana*). (It is interesting to notice that the latter term is in current use on Indian Railways; certain carriages on air-conditioned overnight expresses are designated 'kursi-yana', that

21

is, 'seat-cars', as opposed to sleeping-cars.) The name Mahayana was adopted deliberately, in order to distinguish the new
type of Buddhism and its philosophy from the older type, which
in its turn was characterised by the innovators the 'Hina-yana',
or little vehicle. The basic difference was that the Mahayana was
more consciously universalistic; it was not content with the old ar-
rangement in which the role of lay people was simply to support
the monks, attend the monastery, pay cultic respect to the
Buddha and keep the moral code in the hope of a better rebirth; it
emphasised instead that it was possible for lay people to avail
themselves directly of the help of supernatural saviours known as
Bodhisattvas.

The Bodhisattva is thought of as a being who, upon the threshold of nirvana, deliberately sets aside entry into this final blissful
state out of compassion for the mass of ordinary beings. Instead of
becoming fully Buddha, he remains in the temporal realm in
order to devote himself to the salvation of others. This emphasis
upon compassion which the Bodhisattva concept represents was
not something radically new. Compassion for others had been
regarded as a virtue in earlier Buddhism, but it had there a somewhat subordinate place to wisdom. In the Mahayana development it came to receive an equal emphasis with wisdom, as a
principal virtue in the spiritual ideal which the Bodhisattva represented. Even this, however, was a recovery of what the earlier
spiritual ideal, the arahat, had represented—that is, a man who
had transcended the limiting notion of 'self' and who because of
this was a source of beneficent moral and spiritual influence. The
arahat ideal had become corrupted in the centuries immediately
before the rise of the Mahayana, and needed to be given this new
formulation.

The Bodhisattva was thought of also as a being no longer subject to the physical limitations of human life. He inhabited a
'celestial' realm, a spiritual 'field' brought into being by his own
saintliness. It was into this blessed realm of being that he was
believed to be able to bring others by his spiritual power. There
was in theory no necessary limit to the possible number of Bodhisattvas, and there thus developed belief in a number of such
beings, each known by his own name. Some of the more prominent of these were Avalokiteshwara ('he who looks down in
mercy'), Amitabha ('boundless light') and Manjushri. For lay
people in India of this period each of these became the central

figure in a cult which, phenomenologically, was very similar to the cult of a deity. In this way Mahayana Buddhism provided a transition from indigenous cults of local Indian deities to Buddhist doctrines and practice.

3 Buddhist decline in India

Explanations of Buddhist decline

Whatever view is taken of the decline in the number of Buddhists in India, both monks and lay people, over the past eight centuries one has, it seems, to start from the undeniable fact that Buddhism in India was popular. The name Mahayana itself is an indication of this. The Mahayana was the vehicle 'for the people', it was the comprehensive way. By the use of this term its adherents affirmed the difference in principle between their way and the way of the spiritual elite, the Hinayana.

We have seen that there are severe difficulties in trying to maintain that Buddhism in India simply changed its form and continued undiminished in some new guise. This leaves the possibility that although it disappeared from view its continuing influence was still felt, and that from time to time its spirit finds re-expression in Indian life. Such a view is very close to, but not identical with, the supposition that Buddhism is waiting at the geographical and cultural fringes of India for the favourable opportunity which will enable it to spread back once again into its old heartlands.

Beyond these views, however, there is the possibility that Buddhism *really died*, and that it did so because in the main culture area of India it could no longer maintain itself. This carries the implication that unless there is some radical change in Indian culture Buddhism can never come to life again in this area.

This possibility has now to be examined. Various accounts of the death of Indian Buddhism have been constructed. There are, broadly, four which have been persistently offered, both from within India and from outside. They are as follows:

1 Buddhism died of old age.

2 It came to rely too exclusively on royal support, and died out when this was no longer forthcoming.
3 Its vitality ran out into the sands of popular culture, and it was smothered and died;
4 It suffered from a corruption within its own blood-stream, so to speak (Tantra), and died of self-poisoning.

We shall consider these explanations and shall endeavour to show that as they stand, they are unsatisfactory, that they do not answer the question, but merely raise other equally difficult questions.

That Buddhism in India died of old age is the reason most frequently advanced by Edward Conze, in his *Short History of Buddhism*, for example, and elsewhere. In its usual form it is expressed as an analogy with the human body. Bodies grow old, wear out, and die; and so did Buddhism. The ideas had grown old; they had outlived their usefulness. Just as there is nothing so powerful, so it is said, as an idea when its time is come, so also (it is implied) there is nothing so feeble as an idea when its time is past. A variant of this answer is that 'Buddhism had served its purpose, and there was nothing more left for it to do'. Some picturesque details are sometimes offered in this touching story of Buddhism's death in India: Buddhism expired, 'and was absorbed into the eternally patient, waiting arms of Hindu theism', according to one Hindu writer,[1] or died 'to be born again into a refined Brahmanism' is the curious application of the theory of rebirth offered by another.[2] These are not explanations, but romantic and somewhat rhapsodic analogies. They suffer from the limitations which beset all analogical reasoning (especially bad analogy) that while they may, if they have some appropriateness, stimulate thought, they do not in themselves *explain* anything, and may in fact mislead.

The idea that Buddhism declined in India because of the loss of royal support on which it had come to rely certainly appears more plausible. But, in this case, one has to ask what is being referred to in the word 'Buddhism'. In such contexts it is generally used to mean the Buddhist culture of the classical Sinhalese kingdom with its triangular internal structure: Sangha–king–people. To say that such Buddhism declined for loss of royal support therefore means that the Sangha and the Buddhist lay people were unable to maintain their Buddhist life and culture if the ruler was not a Buddhist. In fact, such a situation is not unknown in the history of

Buddhism: it happened more than once in Ceylon, and also in Burma, in the nineteenth and twentieth centuries. It is true that the patronage of kings greatly assists the *establishing* of Buddhism in a country. It is true also that the rule of a Buddhist monarch has, at various periods, enabled Buddhism to maintain optimal conditions for the maximum number of people to live the Buddhist life. But it is not true to say that Buddhism cannot survive the loss of royal patronage, for it has done so, sometimes for long periods. Buddhist life and culture can more readily survive the loss of royal support than it can the loss of the Sangha. This is the one crucial element, even although, given a sufficiently serious commitment to Buddhism among lay people, even the absence of the Sangha *can* be bridged for short periods. The withdrawal of royal support is, therefore, by itself not a sufficient cause for the absolute disappearance of recognisable Buddhist life such as occurred in Bengal from the eleventh century. This explanation simply moves the question back one stage; it leaves us with the problem: what had become of the Sangha, especially in its relationship with the local people?

This leads on to the third kind of attempt at explanation of Buddhism's disappearance from Bengal: namely, that it was due to excessive popularisation. In this view of things Buddhism was 'corrupted' by popular cults, which it had, apparently, no power to resist. Sir Charles Eliot, for instance, in a chapter entitled 'The decadence of Buddhism in India', after noticing that it was in north-eastern India that Buddhism survived when it had disappeared from north-western, central and southern India,[3] comments that 'Bengal, especially western Bengal and Bihar, was the stronghold of decadent Buddhism'[4] He describes it in the Pala kingdom as 'corrupt', although, he adds, it was flourishing so far as the number of its adherents and royal favour were concerned. He observes that from 700 to 1107 'local superstitions were infecting and stifling decadent Buddhism'.[5] The source of the corruption he identified as Tantrism, whose influence was, in Eliot's view, 'powerful and disastrous'.[6]

Eliot has not been singled out because he is the special representative of this point of view with regard to later Buddhism but because his work has been fairly widely known and influential, and because in writing in this way he was reflecting the judgment of a number of scholars on this period of Indian Buddhist history. Broadly, the assumption has been that it was in Bengal that

Indian Buddhism came to the end of its 1700-year career, some-where around 1200 C.E.; that 'late' Buddhism was Tantric (that is to say, it employed what have been called 'sexo-yogic prac-tices'); that this 'Tantric' Buddhism was 'degenerate'; that Bengal is therefore to be remembered as the home of a form of Buddhism which was late and degenerate, and that largely for these reasons it was the place where Indian Buddhism died.

Buddhism in Bengal

All this might be taken to suggest that there was something in the Buddhism of Bengal that was somehow significantly more 'Ben-gali' than Buddhist, especially if the view is held that Tantric beliefs and practices had originated in Bengal.[7] It might be sup-posed that in Bengal Buddhism was subject to local cultural influ-ences of a significantly different kind, which caused it to develop a new and unhealthy strain. Against this idea—that Bengal had some special modifying effect on Buddhism—certain con-siderations need to be emphasised. They are (1) that the Buddhist presence in Bengal was not confined to the later period, but was represented there at least from the time of Ashoka; (2) that the original ideas, structure and emphases of early Buddhism were in essence preserved faithfully down to the time when the Pala dynasty came to an end; and (3) that the maintenance of an open frontier between Buddhist doctrine and practice on the one hand, and local indigenous popular cults on the other, is a familiar fea-ture of Buddhism (even Theravada Buddhism) throughout its his-tory. In the triangular structure of Sangha, king and people referred to in the first chapter, the role of the Sangha in relation to lay people is mainly that of providing an inspiring moral example which helps the people to keep their own moral goals high (an il-lustration of the principle enunciated by Durkheim: 'It is neces-sary that an elite put the [moral] end too high, if the crowd is not to put it too low')[8] while in recognition of their highly honourable place and function in society, the Sangha receive from the mass of the people the material necessities of life.

Apart from instructing the people in the Buddhist ethic, the monk, like the Buddha himself, shows an unusual tolerance where folk beliefs and practices are concerned. The householder may continue to believe in demons and spirits, in the local gods, or in some supreme god such as Brahma or Sakka. When he is ready to pass beyond such beliefs he will. Until then it is foolish to attempt to force him or to persuade him. Imposed theological or credal orthodoxy is not a feature of the *classical* pattern of Buddhist culture, although there have been attempts of that kind in the modern period. From the very beginning of Buddhist history the lay people who surrounded and supported the Sangha held a variety of beliefs in non-human, celestial beings. Beliefs of this kind have no bearing on the Buddhist scheme of salvation, except that their prominence in the tradition and literature at any given time suggests that the Sangha, far from being cut off from the world in its own private search for salvation is, on the contrary, in lively contact with the common people. This is how the Buddhist scheme appears to work best. There is a frontier between the *prototype society* of those who have overcome the false notion of self with all its consequences, or are seriously engaged in doing so, and the much larger area of *existing society* which has as yet not experienced even the beginnings of this Visuddhi or purification, and it is this frontier which has to be kept open so that there can be free intercourse back and forth. In other words, the prominence of popular beliefs within the Buddhist tradition at any given period will be an indication that the scheme is working well, rather than the reverse.

It is with these considerations in mind that we can now approach the history of Buddhism in Bengal. What will now be apparent is that the question of decadence has been wrongly defined by Eliot and those others who have regarded medieval Buddhism in Bengal as decadent. The implication is that in belief and practice the Buddhism of Bengal in the latter part of the Pala period had fallen away from the purity of the earlier, presumably Magadhan, forms. This is not what the available evidence suggests.

It is along the northern side of the Ganges, as it flows through central Bengal (in what is now Bangladesh) that most of the ancient sites of Bengal Buddhism are to be found. It is here that most of the kingdoms of Bengal in the ancient and medieval periods had their capitals: Gaudha (or Gaur), Mahasthan, Vikrampur and Pattikera. There is, however, one important Buddhist site to the west of the Bhagirati–Hooghly river, and that is the ancient port of Tamralipti.

This port (modern Tamluk, approximately thirty-five kilometres south-west of Calcutta), provides a clear link with the

Ashokan period. It was from this port in Bengal, according to the Mahavamsa, that the Buddhist mission from Ashoka's capital city, Pataliputra, sailed for Ceylon to establish the Sangha in that island. It is an ancient city, mentioned in a number of early Sanskrit sources,[9] and was fairly certainly within the territory of Ashoka's empire. There is other, epigraphic, evidence which points to the conclusion expressed in 1958 by G. M. Bongard-Levin that 'the fact that Bengal was part of the Maurya empire has been finally established'.[10] Similarly, Barrie M. Morrison has recently recorded that 'during the third century BC the Mauryan empire exercised political control [in the delta] as is evidenced by the Brahmi inscription of Pundranagora'. He adds that from excavations at that site in central Bengal, north of the Ganges (known also as Mahasthan), 'many Mauryan coins and other artifacts datable in the fourth and third centuries BC have been recovered' and that this, with textual evidence of various kinds, confirms the view that the delta 'was under the control of the Mauryan empire'.[11] In the view of W. W. Hunter the people of western Bengal were familiar with Buddhism long before they came under the influence of Brahmanism. 'Buddhism,' he wrote, 'was the first form of an elaborated religious belief which the Bengali people received.'[12] Hunter's view is wholly in keeping with the evidence which has accumulated since then, some of which has just been noted, that Bengal was part of the Mauryan empire. With the officers and administrators from Ashoka's court there went, as we know, the members of the Buddhist Sangha into every corner of the Mauryan empire, to make known the Dharma and establish the Sangha. It could hardly have been otherwise in Mauryan Bengal.

The Buddhism which Bengal first received would, therefore, have been the kind whose basic structure we have noted. Under the political rule of one who was himself a Buddhist sympathiser and supporter and who conformed as closely as any ruler could to the ideal king of the Pali texts, the Sangha in Bengal would have been free to play its proper role as adviser and moral guide to the ruler and his officers, and also to expand steadily and unhindered, a process which would have been facilitated by the favourable climate provided by a just and benevolent government. For in many respects Ashoka's kingdom was more nearly a welfare state than anything India has experienced since, until modern times.

The mass of the people outside the Sangha would have continued to adhere to their local forms of belief and mythology, which at this period in Bengal were probably as yet un-Aryanised and of a generally Dravidian character. But from contact with the members of the Sangha which was now established among them they would have gained glimpses of a different view of life which would in the course of time—as it has in other countries with a living Buddhist tradition—have modified their outlook on life and gradually influenced their moral conduct. It would, moreover, have led a certain proportion of them into membership of the Sangha itself. At the end of the fourth century CE the Chinese pilgrim Fa Hsien visited Bengal in the course of his travels in India. Then, as in Ashoka's time, the principal port seems to have been Tamralipti (Tamluk).

> From Champa [now eastern Bihar], journeying east about fifty *yojanas*, Fa-hsien arrived at the country of Tamluk, where there is a seaport. In this country [i.e. region] there were twenty-four monasteries, all with resident *bhikkhus*, and the Buddhist faith is very flourishing. Fa-hsien stayed here for two years, copying out sutras and drawing pictures of images.

At the end of his stay he took passage on a large merchant vessel and after fourteen days reached Ceylon.[13]

It is clear that Buddhism had expanded throughout Bengal by this time. Out of a considerable body of evidence one example may be given. This is a copper plate inscription found at Gunaighar in Tipperah (modern Tripura, on the extreme eastern edge of Bengal, north of Chittagong). The inscription dates from 507 CE and from the references to the monastery it is evident that there had been time for the place to have become old and in need of repair. A gift of land was being made by Vainyā Gupta:

> To Acarya Santideva, the Buddhist monk of Mahayana school, in order that perfume, flowers, lights, incense, etc., for [the worship of] Lord Buddha thrice a day may be provided perpetually in the abode of the Buddhist monks of Vaivarttika sect of Mahayana school, constructed by him [Santideva] in the Vihara, dedicated to Avalokitesvara, and garments, food, bed, seats and medicines for diseases may be supplied to the host of monks, and also in order that breaks and cracks in the

30

monastery may be repaired.[14]

From this and other evidence it is clear that by the fifth century of the Christian era Buddhism, both of the Hinayana and of the Mahayana modes, was known in Bengal as far as the extreme eastern borders. We are not concerned here to consider the respective claims of each of these two modes to represent more faithfully than the other the essence of the Buddhist way. The allegation we are concerned with concerns only Tantric Buddhism, and the view that this was corrupt Buddhism, specially characteristic of Bengal. Since Tantrism does not come on to the Buddhist scene in Bengal in any recognisable way until the time of the Pala kings (eighth to twelfth centuries) it is clear that Buddhism must have existed a long time in Bengal before it became (allegedly) 'corrupt'. This is not to say that forms of belief and practice of a Tantric or sexo-yogic kind cannot be found before the Pala period; indeed, some scholars have seen the roots of such practices in the Indus Valley civilisation of the third and second millennia BC. So far as the adoption of Tantric practices by Buddhists are concerned, L. Joshi has shown that 'the historical beginnings of Buddhist esoterism (Tantrism) go back at least to the first century BC'. He adds that Tantrism seems to have influenced certain sections of the Buddhist Sangha some centuries before Asanga composed the Prajnaparamita sadhana.[15] Asanga, it will be remembered, was from Gandhara in the north-west of India. It is clear that the weight of evidence regarding the areas in which Tantric Buddhism first emerged shows that the north-west and the south of India share this distinction. No places in Bengal are referred to, in so many ancient and medieval texts, as centres of esoteric Buddhism, as are Sriparvata, Dhanyakataka and Potalaka in South India.[16]

The evidence of the Chinese pilgrims and Taranatha

Thus, there is no lack of information about Buddhism in Bengal in the period before the rise of the Pala kings. The Chinese pilgrims Hiuen Tsiang and I-Tsing also visited Bengal in the course of their travels in the seventh century CE, and both commented fairly fully on the state of Buddhism there at that time. By the time Hiuen Tsiang made his journey, in the second quarter of the seventh century, Buddhism was declining in many areas of India outside Bengal—declining, that is to say, in the number of monasteries and in the degree of support and approval it was receiving from rulers. This was especially true of parts of north-west India, such as Gandhara (whose monasteries, as described by Hiuen Tsiang, were ruined and deserted) and the south of India.

In Bengal and Assam Tsiang visited five 'countries' and reported on the state of Buddhism in each of these. The first place he visited was the kingdom of Pundravardhana, in central Bengal to the north of the Ganges and to the west of the Meghna river.[17] Its capital is better known by the later name of Mahasthan. The country around the capital was thickly populated, wrote Hiuen Tsiang, its rich soil producing all kinds of grain and good supplies of fruit. The people were said to 'esteem learning'. There were about twenty monasteries, with a total of about 3,000 monks who adhered to both Hinayana and Mahayana. In addition he found about a hundred temples belonging to various religious groups of whom the Jains were the largest. A few miles to the west of the capital was the great monastery called the Bhasu Vihara, a splendid place with courts, 'light and roomy' and well furnished with lofty towers and pavilions. About 700 monks of the Mahayana lived there, including some whose names were famous throughout eastern India. Hiuen Tsiang then visited the kingdom of Kamarupa in what is now Assam. After this he came to the country of Samatata—that is, the part of Bengal which lies to the east of the Meghna river, down to the borders of Burma. The land was low-lying and rich in crops; 'the flowers and fruits grow everywhere'. The climate was soft, and the manners of the people agreeable. The men were hardy, of small height and dark complexion; 'they are fond of learning and exercise themselves diligently in the acquirement of it'. He found there thirty or more monasteries, all of the Theravadin school. There were also many temples of other cults, the Jains again forming the majority. Near the capital was a stupa, also said to have been built by Ashoka.

Going westward from Samatata (possibly by sea) the pilgrim came to Tamralipti, the port of western Bengal. Here, too, he found a fertile and bountiful land, whose people he describes as 'quick and hasty . . . hardy and brave'. There were about ten monasteries and about a thousand monks. Again he found a stupa built by Ashoka.[18] The last place he visited in Bengal was Karnasuvarna, on the Bhagirathi river, a little south of the modern Berhampore. Here, too, the area of the capital city was thickly populated and the people were very prosperous. There were ten or so monasteries, and about 2,000 monks of the Hinayana. There were about fifty other temples, and non-Buddhists were very numerous. There was also, however, a large monastery just outside the city in which congregated 'all the most distinguished, learned, and celebrated men of the kingdom'. They strove, writes Hiuen Tsiang, 'to promote each other's advancement by exhortations, and to perfect their character', or to take the literal meaning of his words 'to promote their mutual perfection by shaping and smoothing (in the sense of polishing) their reason and virtue'.[19] This provides interesting evidence that the function of the sangha as it appears in early Buddhism was still being maintained in Bengal in the seventh century.

In the middle of the seventh century, soon after the time of Hiuen Tsiang's visit, a period of political chaos occurred when Bengal was the scene of rivalry and struggle among local rulers. This came to an end around the year 750 with the election of Gopala as king, and the founding of the Pala dynasty which was to rule Bengal for about four centuries. The Pala kings were supporters of the Sangha, both in Bengal and in Bihar, where also their territory extended.[20] The Pala period was one of considerable building of Buddhist monasteries: for instance the large monastic complex at Paharpur (just north of modern Santahar) does not appear to have been in existence at the time when Hiuen Tsiang was travelling in this part of Bengal. It has been identified as the great Somapura *vihara* founded by the second of the Pala kings, Dharmapala (c. 770–810).[21] It was well maintained throughout the succeeding three centuries and recent archaeological evidence indicates that it was a flourishing, prosperous and influential Buddhist centre in the twelfth century. It is, observes Dr Hussain, 'the largest single monastic building so far discovered in the whole of the Indian sub-continent'.[22] The memory of its prosperity is preserved in references to Somapura which are found in Tibetan Buddhist writings of the early seventeenth century.

During the period of Pala rule in northern, central and western Bengal the life of the common people appears to have been simple but comfortable. The evidence of copper-plate inscriptions of this period suggests, however, that it was in the south-east of Bengal, in the kingdom of Sumatata, that the Buddhist Sangha found even

33

stronger support than in the Bengal of the Palas. This south-eastern region was ruled by the Chandras, a dynasty of five generations which lasted from the beginning of the tenth century to the middle of the eleventh. One of these, at least, Ladara Chandra, is known from the evidence of inscriptions to have been a Buddhist. His reign (1000–1020) which was devoted 'entirely to peaceful religious acts' was recorded also as having been a time when the kingdom enjoyed general prosperity and secure condition.[23] Some of the other Chandras appear to have inclined more towards Vaishnavism. However, the Sangha was certainly well represented in this part of Bengal during these centuries, much more strongly than in any other part. The very extensive inscriptional evidence shows that donations of land, etc., to Buddhist monasteries were much more frequent and numerous in this part of Bengal than elsewhere. Morrison's survey of the evidence for the whole of the period between 433 and 1283 CE leads him to the conclusion that 'Vaishnavism was strong in the north, central and eastern parts [of Bengal], while Buddhism was well patronised in the east.'[24] The large number of monasteries in eastern Bengal at this time suggests there must have been strong local support from the people of this thickly populated region.

Another important source for knowledge of Buddhism in Bengal, particularly during the period of the Pala kings (that is from the eighth to twelfth century), is Taranatha's history. It is true, as D. Chattopadhyaya comments, that Taranatha includes much that is of a legendary character, but in spite of this, he 'somehow or other managed to squeeze into this brief work a tremendous amount of solid historical data (and interesting Indian folklore) which are not easy to trace in other available sources'.[25]

Taranatha divides his history into chapters, each chapter dealing with the reign of one king, but sometimes more in the case of less important reigns. In each chapter he mentions the outstanding acarya-s of the period under review. In the chapters dealing with the Pala kings there is frequent mention of two Buddhist schools in particular: Prajna-paramita and Tantra, although he does mention also teachers of Vinaya and Abhidharma. He tells us that in the reign of King Devapala (810–850 CE) Manjusrikirti was a great Vajracarya. In his son Rasapala's reign there was a great acarya whose Tantrika name was Lilavajra, and who 'delivered many sermons on the Tantra-yana . . .' According to

34

Taranatha, King Raspala was succeeded by his son, Dharmapala, who, we are told, accepted as his preceptors the acarya-s Haribhadra and Jnanapada, 'and filled all directions with the Prajna-paramita and the Sri Guhya-samaja'. He built fifty centres for the study of the Dharma, thirty-five of which were for Prajnaparamita. He also built the Vikramasila vihara on the northern bank of the Ganga (possibly somewhere in the region of the Bengal/Bihar border). This had a central temple containing 'a human-size statue of the Mahabodhi', and around it 'fifty-three smaller temples of the Guhya Tantra'. Moreover from the time of this king, says Taranatha, 'the Prajna-paramita was extensively propagated'. The great acarya (Buddha) Jnanapada, one of the king's preceptors, 'consecrated the Vikramasila (vihara) and was appointed the Vajracarya there'. In one of the temples there 'was an image of Heruka and many treatises on Tantra'. According to Taranatha some Ceylon monks residing there declared that these Tantrika treatises were composed by Mara, the evil one, and, indeed, felt so strongly on the subject that they burnt the treatises and smashed the silver images to pieces and used the silver fragments as money. Moreover, they warned the peoples of Bengal who came there to worship that these Tantric doctrines were simply adopted by their exponents as a way of making money, and should be avoided: 'Keep clear of these so-called preachers of the True Doctrine', they advised the lay people. When the king got to hear of this he was about to punish the Ceylon monks, but, Taranatha tells us, they were saved by the acarya. The latter continued to preach, 'most extensively', the five Tantras of the initiates, namely the Samaja, Mayajala, Buddha-samuyoga, Candra-guhya-tilaka and Manjusri-krodha. Special emphasis was put on the teachings of the Guhya-Samaja, and so 'it was very widely spread'.

During the reign of King Mahapala an acarya named Pito introduced the Kalacakra Tantra, and spread its teaching and practice. Another famous Tantrika acarya of the Pala period mentioned by Taranatha was Jetari, who had been taught the Guhya-samaja by his father, a Brahman acarya and who in his turn became a great Tantrika-sastra writer. Yet another, in Canaka's reign, was the acarya Vagisvarakirti who had held office at Vikramasila. He built many centres for the study of the Dharma, including eight for Prajna-paramita and four for Guhya-samaja and one each for three other forms of Tantra. 'He used to preach constantly' these doctrines, we are told. He was also famous for the elixirs which he prepared, by the use of which even the oldest could regain their youth. 'In this way he caused welfare to about five hundred ordained monks and pious house-holders.' In the latter part of his life he went to Nepal and preached there the Tantrayana. He was criticised by most of the people because he had so many consorts. Taranatha relates some highly miraculous events in which the acarya was involved to-gether with two of these consorts, 'a voluptuous dancing girl' and 'a black and violent woman'.

This kind of story, of which other examples of a similar kind occur, no doubt underlie Debiprasad Chattopadhya's view of the condition of Buddhism during the later Pala period. Taranatha, he tells us, left us 'clear indications of the factors that contributed to the decline and fall of Buddhism in India', for it had

> almost completely surrendered precisely to those beliefs and practices, as a direct rejection of which the Buddha himself had preached his original creed . . . [it] bowed down to all these [magical] beliefs and practices, and thus became practically indistinguishable from popular Hinduism so called . . . being an elaborate worship of all sorts of gods and goddesses of popu-lar pantheon—often under new names, but sometimes caring not even to invent any new name for them—and of indulging in all sorts of ritual practices for which the Buddha had himself expressed his unambiguous repulsion.[26]

It thus had no internal justification as the fad of its important and wealthy patrons; with the collapse of wealthy or royal patronage it simply disappeared, there being no 'genuine popular enthusiasm for Buddhism'.

Similar reasons for the decline and disappearance of Buddhism at the end of the Pala period are put forward by R. C. Majumdar in his *History of Ancient Bengal*. First, he says, there was 'the change in the character of Buddhism', a change into 'the mystic forms generally referred to as Vajrayana and Tantrayana'. Second, royal patronage which, he says, was always an important factor in the ascendancy of religious sects, was withdrawn from Buddhists at the end of the Pala period, with the coming of the Sen dynasty, so that Buddhism declined in consequence.[27]

Buddhism and popular cults

The argument thus appears to be that the cause of Buddhism's disappearance from India was (1) that it underwent an internal change in accommodating itself to popular cults, and (2) that it had come to rely on the patronage of rich merchants and kings to such an extent that when this was withdrawn Buddhism had no vitality of its own left, no roots in the life of the people and therefore simply died away.

Such an explanation demands careful scrutiny. In the first place it is important to enquire how the Palas came to be patrons of Buddhism. The founder of the dynasty, Gopala, who emerged from the political chaos of mid-eighth-century Bengal on account of his charisma as a leader is a somewhat shadowy figure. It is not known with certainty whether or not he was a Buddhist. Nor is there any clear explanation of why his son announced himself as a follower of the Buddha. One reason which must certainly be taken seriously is that he did so precisely because Buddhism was so widely and popularly supported throughout Bengal.[28] It had certainly been prospering in the seventh century, as Hiuen Tsang's evidence shows, and there seems no good reason why it should be thought to have declined in the intervening century. Indeed, the accusation against Buddhism in the Pala period appears to be that it became too popular—it approximated too closely to the popular culture of Bengal. Such a view of things accounts satisfactorily for the general nature of Taranatha's account of Pala Buddhism also, namely that it was popularly oriented and received patronage from friendly kings and rich merchants.

This in fact was precisely the kind of situation in which the Buddhist Sangha flourished in other periods, both before and after the Palas, in India and in Ceylon and South-East Asia: an open frontier existed between, on the one hand, highly metaphysical matters dealt with in the Dharma and, on the other, popular contemporary beliefs. We have already noted the Buddha's attitude towards the popular beliefs and practices of the average man—the putthujana—as having been mainly one of his tolerant forbearance; his strictures were reserved for what he regarded as the absurdity, cruelty and wastefulness of the Brahmanical sacrificial system.[29] The same attitude has been transmitted in the Sangha down the centuries and still characterises the traditional

Buddhism of Ceylon and South-East Asia.[30]

There is an inherent contradiction in saying that Buddhism declined because it had accommodated itself too much to popular cults on the one hand, and that it relied solely on royal patronage and not on popular support on the other. There would seem to be much more of a case for saying that it was not so much for lack of popular support that Buddhism declined in eastern India, but rather in spite of such support, or even, precisely because it enjoyed such popular support.

It is quite clear that the structure of Buddhism under the Pala dynasty, and especially in the earlier period, was a good representative example of the classical pattern as can be found in any period of Buddhist history or in any country. When it is alleged that Buddhism in Bengal was 'in decline' in the centuries immediately prior to the Afghan invasions of about 1200 CE, one must question what concept of 'decline' is being used. By using the criteria of an exclusivist and intolerant theistic religion one might make out a case for saying that Buddhism, in so far as it had an open frontier with popular beliefs and practices, was (and always has been) in decline; but these criteria are not relevant to the psycho-social philosophy which was Buddhism.[31] For classical Buddhism to be in a state of decadence or decline would mean that the triangular pattern of relationships between Sangha, king and people was no longer functioning in the traditional way. This cannot be said with any truth to have been the case. There is good evidence that the period of Pala rule in Bengal was, in Morrison's words 'a cultural high point in the pre-Muslim history of eastern India'.[32] The Pala kings exercised a lively patronage of art and literature. The monasteries of Bengal became famous for their learning, and 'an extensive Buddhistic religious and philosophical literature was produced'.[33] According to Taranatha a new and vigorous movement in sculpture began in north-central Bengal in the ninth century. The fame of Bengal's Buddhist culture attracted the attention of the Tibetan kings, and after repeated invitations the famous scholar Atisa eventually arrived in Tibet in the year 1042. Atisa's prestige and authority are said to have been un-paralleled and to have given a new direction to the practice of Buddhism in Tibet. It is significant that one of the main reasons why the Tibetan kings were anxious to invite the Buddhist scholar Atisa (born in East Bengal) was in order 'to combat the freer and coarser interpretations of Tantric theories to which the Tibetans seem to have been particularly drawn.'[34] Atisa in collaboration with an older contemporary Luyi-pada or Lui, had prepared a Buddhist Tantric work, and his collaborator Lui was also the composer of some of the earliest extant poems in Bengali, poems which embody the religious tenets of a form of Tantric Buddhism.

It is clear that the context in which the Tantric ideas and practices which had become a matter of serious interest in the Buddhism of Bengal by the end of the tenth century have to be placed is that of Buddhism's general open-frontier policy towards popular contemporary religious beliefs and practices. The form of popular religious ideas which goes by the name of Tantra was widespread throughout India. Part of this tradition, common throughout various regions of India, centred around what may be described briefly as the mysticism of sexual love, or the transcendence of individuality through the experience of conjugal union. Religious ideas and practices of this sort would appear to have a special appropriateness for Buddhism whose central concern was the transcending of the notion of individual self and the widening of the area of consciousness. A Buddhism that was out of touch with the people would have remained out of touch with these ideas. It is a measure of the liveliness of the contacts between Sangha and people in the Pala period that Tantric ideas were coming within the province of Buddhism, there to be adapted and expressed in ways that could serve the continuing tradition.

So long as the Sangha is alive and well Buddhism does not stand to lose anything from having an open frontier with popular belief and practice. So long as the Sangha, as the bearer of Buddhist values and norms, is present, the traffic to and fro across that frontier is of a kind which strengthens and deepens the Buddhist character of the society. For Bengal society to have changed its character and become un-Buddhistic could only have happened if the Sangha had ceased to be itself, or had disappeared. Once again we find that this explanation of Buddhism's disappearance—that it was lost in popular folk-lore—is by itself no explanation; it simply poses the prior or more basic question, what then, had become of the Sangha?

The hostility of Brahmans

We turn, therefore, to a fourth possible explanation and one which does address itself to this basic question. It concerns the hostility of the Brahmans towards the Sangha, and is an explanation which has occurred to more than one historian of Indian religion. It has recently been set out with an impressive amount of supporting evidence by Lalmoni Joshi.[35] He points to evidence of the fact of Brahmanical hostility to Buddhism teaching and unwillingness to share royal patronage and cultural influence with Buddhist monks.

The Manava-sastra and Kautilya's Artha-sastra afford plenty of evidence of this kind of attitude. The stronger the raj, the more important it became for Brahmans to establish and maintain their own position at court and in the kingdom at large. On the other hand, in a period when there was no strong, extensive rule, such as the century between the time of Hiuen Tsiang and the beginning of the Pala rule, a period characterised later, in the Khalimpur copper-plate of Dharmapala, as matsyanyayam,[36] it is easy to see that the Buddhist Sangha was less likely to be dislodged, by Brahmanical rivals, from the position of popularity which it held in Hiuen Tsiang's time. To have done so the Brahmans would in such circumstances have needed a powerful political ally, and this was not to be had during that century. Buddhism could therefore be expected to continue at the same level of popular esteem and support into the eighth century, when Gopala established his rule in Bengal.

By the time the Muslim conquest of Bengal began, soon after the year 1200, the sangha no longer held the position which it had enjoyed at the beginning and throughout the Pala period. The crucial period is evidently the century and a half between the end of effective Pala rule and the displacement of Laksmana Sen by the Muslim invaders in 1206. If Buddhist institutions had declined so noticeably during the Sen period—that is, between about 1050 and 1200—it is not unreasonable to assume that the cause of the decline is to be found in some feature which was present in Bengal during the Sen period but not in the Pala perioc One does not have to look very far to find it. The Sens, unlike the Palas, were not Bengalis; they were South Indians and upholders of the Brahmanical system. The persecution and harrying of Buddhists by Brahmanical rulers both in north and south India at this period of Indian history is far from unknown. The anti-Buddhist activities of Sasanka in north India and of Kumarila Bhatta, for example, in south India, could not, in spite of modern

Brahmanical attempts to overlook them,[37] have been other than severely damaging to Buddhist life and institutions, as, in accordance with the injunctions of Manava Sastra, they were no doubt meant to be. Similarly, the Sen dynasty in Bengal constituted a menace to the survival of Buddhist life, a menace which soon became a reality. The Sens, coming from the conservative and orthodox Deccan, were unlikely to perpetuate the social liberalism which had been encouraged during the Buddhist Pala period. The society the Sens created was one in which caste differences were emphasised and upheld, and in which a multitude of state officials flourished at the expense of both the peasantry and the merchants. The latter were, traditionally, prominent supporters of the Buddhist Sangha, and their decline during the Sen period would inevitably have had the effect of further depressing the Buddhists, now already a depressed section of Bengal society under Pala rule.

Those who reject the view that it was orthodox Brahmanism which brought about the decline of Buddhism in Bengal in the Sen period[38] offer as an alternative explanation of this decline (which, quite clearly, has to be explained somehow), the idea that Buddhism had become 'exhausted' by some sort of natural process of 'old age'. It was old and tired, and having no means of rejuvenating itself, it just died; such is the explanation offered. It 'merged' into Brahmanism, or, in S. Radhakrishnan's words, as was noted earlier, 'perished in India', to be born again in a refined Brahmanism.[39] This is not exactly the language of professional historiography. Such fanciful and figurative use of the idea of being 're-born', is, in fact, a way of saying it was succeeded by a renovated Brahmanism, or simply that it was replaced by Brahmanism. Radhakrishnan is aware that this statement is, in any case, true only of India. Buddhism, although equally 'old' anywhere else in the world, did not expire outside India as it did within India. It did not die in Ceylon in the thirteenth century, or in Burma, or in Thailand, although it did run into difficulty, however, in Brahmanical Sumatra and Java and Malaya. Significantly these were the lands which also afterwards became Islamic. Burma and Siam, which remained strongly Theravadin Buddhist, resisted Islamic expansion. As in Bengal, it was not Islam which overcame Buddhism, but a more jealous rival of nearer origin.

Certain other considerations are important in this connection which there is only the space to mention briefly. The Muslims who invaded Bengal from the beginning of the thirteenth century onwards did not distinguish or discriminate between Brahmanical and Buddhist religion; to them, all were 'Hindu'—that is, 'Indian' or non-Muslim. There is evidence that the relations between Buddhists and Muslims were, if anything, slightly more friendly than between other 'Hindus' and Muslims. The fourteenth-century Muslim traveller, Ibn Battuta, in his account of Ceylon, writes concerning the Buddhists that 'they show respect for Muslim darwishes, lodge them in their houses, and give them to eat, they live in their houses amidst their wives and children.' This is contrary, he adds, 'to the usage of the other Indian idolaters who never make friends with Muslims, and never give them to eat or to drink out of their vessels.'[40] If the Brahmans managed to survive the Muslim occupation of Bengal, the Buddhists could be expected to have survived also—had they still maintained the position in Bengal life they had held before the coming of the Sens. The disappearance of the Buddhists from Bengal could be attributed directly to the Muslim invasion only if Brahmanism also had perished at the hands of the Muslims; the latter were hardly likely to have extended special favours to the Brahmans which they withheld from the Buddhists. If both Brahmanism and Buddhism had undergone the Islamisation of Bengal on equal terms, Buddhism could be expected to have survived at least equally as well as Brahmanism. This was not the case, and the only reasonable inference is that Buddhism had already been severely crippled before the Muslims reached Bengal.

As for the dying-of-old-age explanation, this is falsified by the evidence from South-East Asian Buddhism. A Western Buddhologist, Edward Conze, sees the history of Buddhism down to the present in terms of five periods of five hundred years. The first three of these periods—namely 500 BC to 0, 0 to AD 500, and 500 to 1000 C.E., each has its own characteristic development in Buddhist thought and practice, namely, the Old Wisdom School, the Mahayana and the Tantra. But the latter two periods from 1000 C.E. to the present show no new development, says Conze. This is perhaps a somewhat Indocentric view. In South-East Asian Buddhism the period 1000 to 1500 C.E. was characterised by the emergence of the South-East Asian Buddhist kingdom; such were the Buddhist kingdoms of Burma, Siam, Laos and Cambodia. These were, as nearly as has ever been achieved (and to a greater degree than in India even under Asoka), Buddhistic civilisations, with no serious internal rival ideology (as had been the case in India), societies where Buddhist values permeated deep into the national life. Indeed it was for this civilising and culture-bestowing quality that Buddhism was originally welcomed in South-East Asia.[41] Evidently, Buddhism was not dying of old age in the thirteenth century. Moreover, the most recent 500-year period has also seen a new characteristic developing in Buddhism. This is the period from 1500 to the present, of contact with European civilisation and thought. The effect was most clearly seen in Siam and Ceylon. In Siam, King Mongkut's modernising reform of the Sangha and of Buddhist thought and teaching did much to reinvigorate Siamese Buddhism and bring it into the twentieth century well equipped to meet the demands of the time. In Ceylon the emergence of what may very broadly be called a trend towards a layman's Buddhism has been the most notable feature, although it is still difficult to analyse properly. Nevertheless, there is sufficient evidence that Buddhism had not by the thirteenth century necessarily come to a developmental dead-end, so that all that remained for it was a graceful demise and 'rebirth' into Brahmanism. If this was untrue of Buddhism in South-East Asia it was in principle untrue of Buddhism in Bengal. It was not old age that killed Buddhism in Bengal, nor was it the arrival of Islam; nor, most certainly, was it because Buddhism in Bengal had by the eleventh century ceased to be popular; rather it had become too popular in a situation where such popularity was dangerous.

In connection with the rapidity with which the Islamisation of eastern Bengal appears to have occurred it is important to bear in mind that the Brahmanisation of society had not always been welcomed by those who had been subjected to it. This is still the case, for the prospect of living at the lowest level of a hierarchical society, as a member of a depressed caste, is not a great incentive to conversion to Hindu religion. Thus, even today 'tribal' (that is non-Hindu) people such as the Santals are known to be strongly resistant to the blessings of the *Sanatana dharma*. The designations 'tribal' and 'low caste' convey the sense that those to whom these terms are applied are somehow inferior human beings. In fact, their only 'inferiority' may often turn out to be that they made the mistake of not being born as caste Hindus, if inferiority is measured by any other than caste criteria. Physically the non-Hindu, non-Brahman inhabitant of India may be the superior;

intellectually also he or she is not necessarily inferior to the Brahman if given equally good opportunities of education and development, as can be seen in the cases of those members of tribal societies who have become not low-caste Hindus but Muslims or Christian or Buddhist, or who have become educated tribal or hill people.

It is therefore not surprising that when alternative routes to social and cultural progress have been open to them, other than into Hindu society, tribal and hill people have chosen to take them. So also at certain earlier periods of Indian history did those who were at the lowest levels of Hindu society. The expansion of Muslim rule in north India was one such period, and perhaps the most notable.

One other factor has to be kept in mind here. Brahmanical hostility towards the Buddhist Sangha would have a better chance of succeeding in its aim, that of dislodging the Sangha from their position of respect and influence, if the common people were, for some reason, not in a position to be able to support the Sangha when it was under attack. In Ceylon on certain occasions when the Sangha was under attack from a non-Buddhist king and his queen, the people declared their support for the Sangha even when the latter had been turned out of their chief monastery by the king. In time the weight of popular opinion and the practical support which the people gave in maintaining the Sangha brought about a reversal of policy and the re-instatement of the Sangha to its former place in Sinhalese society.[42] In Bengal, however, during the period we are considering, that is, during Sen rule in the latter part of the twelfth century, until the coming of the invading Muslims in 1206, there may have been a special reason why popular support for the Sangha faltered. It is a reason which I have suggested tentatively, elsewhere;[43] it concerns the economic basis of the Sangha's continued existence, and is a matter which is important for understanding why Buddhism spread into some areas of South-East Asia and not into others.

The support of a community of monks who are themselves debarred by the regulations of their order from engaging in economic activities, and even from putting spade to earth, requires an available surplus of resources of food and other material necessities, however modest, which the rest of society are prepared to devote to the upkeep of the monks. The lands of Indianised Asia in which Buddhism has flourished are those which, down to the

present time have not suffered from the problems of over-
population. Burma, Thailand, Laos and Cambodia have, until
very recently, had remarkably low population densities and rich
food resources compared with many other countries of Asia, and
compared with Bengal especially. It is possible that the balance
between food production and population was not yet critical in
Bengal in the medieval period, *given normal conditions of life.* But the
one kind of factor which makes all the difference may well have
been the anti-Buddhist policy of the Sen rulers. Then, added to
this, would have been the adverse economic conditions created by
the influx of the invading Muslims. Armies did their campaigning
in India in the dry season, after the rice harvest. At that time the
cultivators of Bengal would have gathered the season's paddy into
their barns, to use through the coming year until the next harvest.
If just at that time an army descended on the countryside, needing
food, for horses as well as for men, this would have made very
heavy inroads into the accumulated stocks, for such armies had no
base in the rear supplying them with food and equipment; they
lived off the land. The economic life of the countryside suffered accordingly, and if there was no longer any surplus, and possibly
even a problem of how villagers were to survive until the next harvest, the Sangha would have been placed in a very vulnerable position.

This was the situation in Bengal throughout most of the thirteenth century as the Muslim invaders made their way eastward,
district by district, year by year. Once this critical situation had
been reached all the forces detrimental to the survival of Buddhism would have been brought into play. Loss of popular support
because of economic shortage would have denied to the Sangha
the chance of being popularly maintained. The hostility of the
Brahmans towards the Sangha would then have been able to come
fully into play. They would have been the least likely to come to
the rescue of the Buddhist monks whose monasteries were being
plundered by Muslim troops; rather the reverse. With the Sangha
disordered and dispersed, popular cults would gradually take
over, and Buddhist values be ignored and forgotten, just as the
ruined deserted monasteries were quickly overgrown by the ad-
vancing tropical jungle.

Thus, the following conclusions are suggested:

1. The greater part of the decline of Buddhism took place after

the end of the Pala period and before the coming of the Muslims, under the Brahmanical Sen regime.

2. The final blow was the indirect economic disability produced by the arrival in Bengal of invading Muslim troops living off the land, thus rendering popular economic support of the Sangha impossible to maintain.

4 Buddhism in India today

The secular nature of the Republic of India

In the previous chapter it was suggested that Brahmanical hostility was a principal cause of Buddhism's disappearance from India. If not all Brahmans, then certainly a powerful section of that class evidently regarded Buddhism as objectionable, for whatever reason. It is not difficult to see that the close ties which could develop between the Sangha and the political ruler would have been a prime source of Brahmanical hostility. While a ruler might, as Ashoka did, try to extend patronage to both Brahmans and Buddhists, this was not an easily maintained stance. More often rulers perceived important differences between the two philosophies and favoured one at the expense of the other. If a ruler was ever in any doubt on the matter Brahmans as a class would usually have been able to bring powerful persuasion to bear. Some kings perceived the value of the Sangha as a possible aid to social control and the enhancement of attitudes of peaceableness among the people, an aid which was less costly than the service provided by large companies of Brahman priests. Buddhist monks did not claim to command supernatural forces, nor were they likely (as were Brahmans) to invoke supernatural sanctions. They relied on the goodwill of the people, the attractiveness and simplicity of their teaching and the uprightness of their own conduct. Of course there were exceptions, but these were the broad general characteristics of Buddhist monks compared with Brahman priests.

If the essence of the disability which Buddhism suffered in India was the hostility of the Brahmans, concerned as the latter were for the preservation of the Brahmanical type of state, then the disappearance of the latter in the modern period beyond any apparent possibility of its revival should, it seems, mean the removal of

47

Buddhism's disability in India. Now that the Republic of India has been established as a secular state, and now that the lion-headed column, the symbol of the Ashokan empire, and the wheel which is the symbol of the Buddha-Dharma have been adopted by the government of India as its own, the prospects for Buddhism in India might be considered to have improved. But there are other factors than the setting up of a secular state to be considered. First, however, we must consider the nature and the extent of the Buddhist presence in India.

Buddhism in modern India: a survey

There were nearly four million Buddhists in India in 1971.[1] The largest group was in the state of Maharashtra. The rest of India's Buddhists were located in two main areas: in the north-east—in the area lying east of a line drawn from Sikkim to Calcutta—and in the *north-west*, in Jammu and Kashmir and parts of Himachal Pradesh. The former of these contained about 350,000 (including Sikkim), and the latter about 93,000 Buddhists. Another 100,000 were distributed widely but unevenly throughout the rest of India.[2]

The group of more than three million in Maharashtra and neighbouring districts is, as we noted earlier, of recent growth, mainly since the conversion of Ambedkar in 1956. The actual number may be greater than the figure just mentioned for, as Zelliott comments, 'Buddhists themselves claim that the census figures are not accurate because census-takers prefer to minimise the extent of the conversion'.[3] Whereas the Maharashtra zone now contains the majority of India's Buddhists, in 1931 the situation was very different. In that year the only notable Buddhist population to be found within the territory which now constitutes the Republic of India (that is, excluding Pakistan and Bangladesh) was located in the north-west and the north-east. Roughly two-thirds of the total lived in what is now West Bengal, Assam and Tripura, and about a quarter lived in the Jammu and Kashmir area.[4]

The neo-Buddhists of Maharashtra could perhaps be regarded as an example of *resurgent* Buddhism. Doubts have been expressed, however, as to the quality and possible permanence of the renewal of Buddhist life in that area. Even as early as the year of Dr

48

Ambedkar's official conversion, when many thousands of Untouchables followed him in taking refuge in the Buddha, the Dharma and the Sangha and in accepting the Five Precepts, Taya Zinkin, writing from Bombay was making sceptical observations. Ambedkar's followers would, in her view, 'revert to their own Hindu gods very soon, no matter what pledge they may have taken at his insistence'.

The Untouchables, she wrote, 'have yet to find out that Buddhism will not make them equal citizens, for they will remain untouchable to their caste fellows; they will have left a cosy god of their own for an abstract principle and they will have lost those many educational and economic privileges the caste Hindus are showering on backward people in the attempt to bring them to equality.'[5] Twenty years later some observers seem to be confirming Taya Zinkin's prognostication. B. G. Gokhale has commented that although 'conversions from among the Untouchables continued it was clear that the movement had lost its momentum' after Ambedkar's death in 1956. 'The new Buddhist community was left without leadership, intellectual as well as political, and soon the new Buddhists tended to become another "untouchable" caste especially in the rural areas of Maharashtra. Buddhism had come and gone like a mighty hurricane that swept thousands off their feet only to deposit them, in a manner of speaking, a few yards away on the same level.'[6]

There is other evidence, however, which suggests that it is a mistake to conclude that the Buddhist movement, when it does not take the form of a hurricane, is non-existent. The Report on the 1931 Census of India indicates that a quarter of a century before Ambedkar's conversion the movement, which became sensational for a while in his lifetime, could already be detected in a quieter, steadier form. With regard to Cochin State it was recorded in 1931 that 'most of the Buddhists there are educated Malayali Iruvas who have abandoned Hinduism on account of their social disabilities in that community'.[7] Moreover, at a different social level, there were not lacking, among the sophisticated, those who were conventionally Hindu but who had become alienated from what they saw as caste-ridden obscurantism, and who, like Jawaharlal Nehru, were attracted to Buddhism. B. K. Gokhale records the fact that in the 1920s and 1930s 'a knowledge of Buddhism and an awareness of its contributions to Indian philosophy and culture were gradually becoming a part of the new intellectual movement in Maharashtra', even although he regards this as different in kind from 'a new living religious tradition'.[8] (It was Ambedkar's teacher, K. A. Keluskar, who initially aroused the former's interest by presenting him with a copy of a life of the Buddha when he graduated from high school at the age of 17). It is, however, difficult to make rigid distinctions between 'intellectual movements' and 'living religious traditions'. The significance of the neo-Buddhist movement, with its centre in Maharashtra state will be examined more fully in the following chapters. Meanwhile, we move on to the Buddhist situation in north-east India.

Buddhism in north-east India: Tibetan

First, it is necessary to consider the character of the Buddhist presence in the north-east. This might be regarded as an area where such Buddhist life as there is represents a residue merely of what was once a thriving, living tradition reaching back to the days of Sakyamuni himself. In Bengal and Assam, Buddhism survived longer than almost anywhere else in India (except possibly in parts of the south) until its very rapid decline from about the eleventh century onwards, since when it shrank virtually to nothing. What is left in the remote fringe areas, it might be thought, are the last vestiges of a practically extinct tradition. In order to test this theory it is necessary to look more closely at the distribution of the Buddhist population of the north-east.

In the state of West Bengal in 1971 there were 121,000 Buddhists. Of these, 107,000 were found in two of the state's sixteen districts, namely Darjeeling and Jalpaiguri. These two districts comprise part of the Himalayan foothills and the adjacent strip of the plains immediately below Sikkim and Bhutan. The Buddhists here are predominantly rural dwellers (82 per cent) and consist mainly of Lepchas (the original inhabitants of the Darjeeling area), Bhutanese, Sherpas, Tamangs and Tibetans.

When the hill tract of 138 square miles, which was the nucleus of Darjeeling District, was acquired by the East India Company from the Raja of Sikkim in 1835 it was 'almost entirely under forest and practically uninhabited'.[9] The only inhabitants of these hills and forests were Lepchas, who were possibly about 100 in number. As soon as Darjeeling began to be developed as a hill resort and sanatorium an influx of population began, mainly from neighbouring Nepal, with some also from Sikkim. The eastern portion of Darjeeling District, the Kalimpong sub-division, was annexed as a consequence of the British war with the neighbouring state of Bhutan in 1865. The annexed area had a native population at that time of about 3500, mostly Bhutias; this nucleus, like that of the original portion, was subsequently increased by in-migration from Nepal.

Thus, the three original ethnic groups were Lepcha, Bhutia and Nepali. The question with which we are concerned is whether any of these can claim to be Buddhists in a continuing tradition reaching back to the time before the virtual disappearance of Buddhism from the rest of India.

The Lepchas of the Darjeeling area, according to one account of their origins, were driven southwards out of the higher Himalayas in the seventeenth century by the Tibetans and were again displaced from the western part of what is now Bhutan and Kalimpong by the Bhutanese in the early eighteenth century. They are primarily people of the forests, and have tended also to move away from the neighbourhood of Darjeeling as it became more developed. In Sir James Hooker's account of them (1854) they appear as having only relatively recently become Buddhists: 'The earliest traditions which they have of their history date no further back than some three hundred years, when they describe themselves as having been long-haired, half-clad savages. At about that period they were visited by Thibetans, who introduced Buddha-worship, the plaiting of hair into pigtails and many other of their own customs.'[10] Dalton quotes Dr A. Campbell's note of 1840 to the effect that 'the Lepchas are Buddhists', and that some of their Lamas 'are educated at home' while others 'go for their education to the great monastic establishments beyond the snows [i.e. in Tibet]' and that they have also some Tibetan Lamas.[11] J. A. H. Louis, who travelled in North Bengal and Sikkim in the 1890s, described the Lepchas as 'partially converted to Buddhism' but still clinging 'to old superstitions and old forms of fetishism or demonolatry'. He adds that 'many of the ceremonies of Sikkim Buddhism for the propitiation or subjugation of evil spirits are no doubt of Lepcha origin'.[12] These comments are in the usual style of English Protestant colonial writers; others of the same period would describe Burmese Buddhism as a gross degeneration from the 'pure Buddhism' of the Pali texts. According to another account of their origins the Lepchas 'are supposed to have come from the East along the foothills from the direction of Assam and Upper Burma'. However, even on this view of their origins, it is agreed that so far as their religion was concerned this was introduced 'from Tibet by Lamas from different monasteries who travelled south and converted the people'.[13]

The Bhutias are a community in a cultural and religious sense; they have been described as 'Mongoloid populations of Buddhist faith and Tibetan speech'.[14] Geographically they are found in the higher ranges of the Himalayas both within Tibet, defined politically, and in the border areas to the south which politically are contained within the states of Nepal, Sikkim and Bhutan. The name 'Bhot' or 'Bhut' indicates Tibet, in the cultural sense. Bhutan is so called because it was considered the *anta* or 'end' of Bhut or Tibet (*Bhut-anta*), that is, the extreme eastern end. The term Bhutia, or Tibetan people, can thus mean either those who belong to the land of Tibet as it is now known or those who are of Tibetan religion and culture, but having a homeland in one of the states to the south which have just been mentioned. Thus, they have become known severally as 'Tibetans' or 'Bhutanese' or 'Sikkim Bhutias' or Sherpas. This last term refers to the Bhutias of Nepal; it means 'easterners' and indicates that they live in the eastern part of Nepal, not far from the border with the Darjeeling District of India.

Buddhist beliefs and practices may have been introduced to the Bhutias of Bhutan as early as the eighth century, when the Indian Buddhist teacher Padma Sambhava is said to have visited the country at the invitation of the king of Bhutan, Sindhu Raja, himself an Indian. The tradition is that Guru Padma Sambhava travelled extensively throughout Bhutan, teaching the Dharma and founding *gompas* (monasteries).[15] It is possible, therefore, that the Bhutias of Bhutan represent a continuous, direct tradition of Indian Buddhism. But it is not more than a possibility; no firm evidence in support of a direct Indian tradition is known, and it is generally held that Bhutan received its Buddhism from Tibet.[16] The Bhutias of Sikkim also claim Guru Padma Sambhava as the founder of Buddhism in their country, but its establishment there in the form in which it is now known, as a powerful hierarchical institution, dates only from the mid-seventeenth century (about 1647), when it was introduced from Tibet. It was from this time that many gompas began to be built in Sikkim. And it was at about this time that Buddhism began to be established among the Sherpas of Nepal; again it was from Tibet that it came.

The Nepalis of North Bengal are predominantly Hindu, but among the non-Hindu tribes there are two, apart from the Sherpas, who are Buddhist or partly Buddhist. These are the Tamangs and the Newars.

Of these the Tamangs are numerically the largest in Darjeeling District; they are referred to in some of the older literature as Murmis. Whereas some of the present inhabitants of Nepal are descended from Hindus who moved into the area at the time of Muslim expansion in North India, these three tribes, together with some others, are of Mongolian origin, and have a much longer history in the territory now comprised within the Kingdom of Nepal. The Tamangs may at some very early period have moved here from Tibet; their physical characteristics and the names of their exogamous divisions are said to support this.[17] However, a recent study of Tamang traditions preserved in a (recently published) work in Nepalese, reveals that in the Tamang view of the matter they did not originate in Tibet. It is accepted that Buddhism (*lama dharma*) entered their country from Tibet in the eighth century, at the time of its conquest by the Tibetan King Svangsan Gempo.[18] In Darjeeling District, as also in Jalpaiguri District and Sikkim, where also they are now found, the Tamangs form part of the general Nepali movement into adjacent territories as a result of population explosion and land hunger. In these districts of India they constitute one of the largest Buddhist groups, and provide a centre of Buddhist solidarity for other smaller groups. This is particularly noticeable, for example, in the Darjeeling town area, where the Tamang gompa is a well-known centre of Buddhist life; it was built in 1926 and has received several additions since, and is now used not only by the Tamangs themselves but also by Newar merchants and shopkeepers, by Sherpas and by Bengalis. When I visited it in 1976 it had two resident lamas and three novices, who were living in quarters adjoining the temple, where also there is a primary school. The lamas are supported by the regular contributions of the Tamang Buddhist Association, among whose members are Newars and Sherpas also.

In the District of Darjeeling there are approximately 60,000 Tamangs, of whom 90 per cent are Buddhists; those who are more remote from the town are served by some twenty smaller gompas. The three novices who were in training in the Darjeeling town monastery in 1976 would later go to outlying places, such for example as the monastery at Ging (Lebong) where the lama at that time was an old man of 80. The Tamang gompa in Darjeeling is of the Nyingmapa sect, but Buddhists of other sects also come there for *puja*.[19]

The Newars, who in Darjeeling are known by the surname 'Pradhan' are divided religiously: some are Buddhists, others have become Hinduised—the former are known as *Buddha-margis* and the latter as *Siva-margis*. They come from the central valley area of Nepal around Kathmandu, and were the dominant group there until the fourteenth century. Their original culture appears to have been Buddhist, and it is possible that the Newars have some claim to represent a surviving tradition of Indian Buddhism. It is only with great difficulty, however, that the Buddha-margis among them have preserved this tradition in Nepal, as the English Buddhist, Sangharakshita, who spent some time among them about thirty years ago, has recorded.[20] In Darjeeling, where they work as traders and cultivators, they are able to maintain their Buddhist practices through their association with other Buddhists from Nepal (Tamangs and Sherpas), as we have just noted.

The other notable Bhutia community in north Bengal today are those who have come from Tibet recently. Some of these came to India as traders before the Chinese invasion of Tibet; many more have come since as refugees. In Darjeeling town their common life has a focal point in the Bhutia Basti area, where there is a gompa of some years' standing, a large newly built school for Tibetan refugee children, and a Tibetan refugees' self-help centre where Tibetan arts and crafts are practised and an income derived from the sale of the goods produced.

Bhutias are found, beyond Darjeeling District, to the east of Bhutan, in the Kameng Division of Arunachal Pradesh. They are also found in the valley districts of Assam north of the Brahmaputra, especially in Darrang, which borders Kameng, and in Lakhimpur. In general the Buddhist peopling of this area has been due to a gradual movement of Bhutanese, before and after the British period. Buddhism's introduction and growth in Bhutan is roughly parallel to that of Sikkim.

Tibetan Buddhism: slow growth

If we now consider the Buddhism of the Himalayan and sub-

Himalayan parts of north-east India in general perspective, it is clear that very little if any of it can fairly be regarded as a surviving continuous tradition from the days before the decline of Indian Buddhism. Some is due to the influx of Tibetan refugees in the 1950s and 1960s; this is true mainly of Darjeeling District, but even there the Tibetan refugees can have formed only a relatively small proportion of the 91,358 Buddhists enumerated in the district in the 1971 Census. The question therefore arises whether the fact that Buddhists are found in somewhat greater numbers in Himalayan north-east India than elsewhere (except Maharashtra) can be attributed in some sense to Buddhist *resurgence*. The answer, as I see it, must be equivocal.

In the first place, the presence of Buddhists here is due mainly to migration into the region from the higher Himalaya and from Nepal; it is thus a tradition of Buddhism which comes mainly from Tibet, except in the case of the Newars; but they form only a very small part of the total. In any case the presence of Newars does not affect the general principle which is demonstrated here— namely, that Buddhism has shown its ability to *re-establish* itself on Indian soil in the modern period, once it is reintroduced. This is a principle of some significance, to which we shall return.

Meanwhile, some account has to be taken of the fact that in Himalayan north-east India the Buddhist population is declining in proportion to the rest of the population. Between 1931 and 1951 the total population of Darjeeling District grew by 27·0 per cent but the Buddhist population by only 5·4 per cent. Between 1951 and 1961 the District population growth rate was 41·0 per cent, but the Buddhist growth rate only 32·2 per cent. This was slightly better than the previous twenty years, and was probably due partly to the influx of Tibetan refugees. The rise in the substantive numbers of Buddhists in the district was most steep in the decade 1951–61, as the following table shows:

No. of Buddhists in Darjeeling District

1931	58,934
1951	62,150
1961	82,304
1971	91,358

In the twenty years from 1931 to 1951 the increase in numbers was 3216. In the ten years 1951–61 it was as high as 20,150, but in the following ten years, 1961–71, only 9054. Moreover, from 1931 at least, the rate of growth of the Buddhist population has been lower than the general rate of growth for the total population, as we have seen. That is to say, the Buddhist community has not even been maintaining its relative position. Thus we have to reckon with the fact that although, in this part of India, Buddhism—mainly of a Tibetan form—has succeeded in re-establishing itself by means of migrants who, for a certain period, have been able to maintain a Buddhist presence in India, nevertheless the percentage of Buddhists to the total population has, at least since 1907, declined. In 1907 they formed 18 per cent of the population of the District, and again in 1931 they formed 18.44 per cent; in 1951, 13·96 per cent; in 1961, 13·0 per cent; and in 1971 only 11·68 per cent.[21] This 'decline' is however, only relative to the rates of growth of other religious groups in the population. There has been no substantive decline in numbers, as the table given earlier shows. The fact that Buddhists have grown less rapidly than the adherents of other religions may be accounted for in various ways. In general, growth of population is the result of one or both of two factors. The first is an excess of immigration over emigration. The second is an excess of births over deaths. Hindus, Muslims and Christians in Darjeeling District all have higher population growth rates than Buddhists. This could mean that adherents of these religions have been moving into the district in greater numbers relative to the size of the existing communities than has been the case with the Buddhists. Or it could mean that they have had a greater excess of births over deaths. The cause of such an excess is either high fertility (more children per couple) or a lower death rate, or both. The data available from the Census Reports do not enable us to investigate the extent of inter-religious contrasts of this kind. But elsewhere, also, Buddhist populations have been characterised by slower growth, mainly due to lower fertility and the same could be the case here. Moreover, it is not unlikely that the Catholic Christian population of Darjeeling District would have had a higher fertility rate than the Buddhist. The fertility rate among Hindus and Muslims is also, in general, likely to be higher than among Buddhists, not for directly religious reasons, but owing to the importance, in these two religions, of male progeny, a feature that is generally characteristic of patriarchy and patrilineal systems.[22] Until fieldwork in Darjeeling District on religious differentials in immigration, in mortality and fertility rates has been carried out it is obviously not possible to go beyond *a priori* assumptions of this kind.

Buddhism in north-east India: Burmese

It is not only in the Himalayan area, however, that Buddhists are found in north-east India. Almost as many are contained within the valley and hill regions of Assam and the hill states of Tripura, Mizoram and the eastern part of Arunachal Pradesh. These are the adherents of a tradition of Buddhism which in general is more akin to that of Burma, although in some parts of it is the tradition of Tibet, introduced by Nepali immigrants (even as in a few places in Burma itself where Nepalis have penetrated). In certain districts of Assam the growth rate of the Buddhist population for the decade 1961–71 was higher than that of the general population, notably in Lakhimpur (39·44 per cent as against 35·74 per cent), Darrang (89·37 per cent against 34·62 per cent), and North Cachar Hills (843·75 per cent against 40 per cent). In the new state of Meghalaya it was 85·76 per cent as against 31·5 per cent; and in the West Tripura District of Tripura State it was 44·36 per cent as against 30·94 per cent. The total number of Buddhists in the area covered by the State of Assam grew from the tiny figure of 1,621 given by W. W. Hunter in 1881[23] to about 15,000 in 1931, and since then had grown to more than 90,000 by 1971. This is a much more rapid growth than in the Himalayan region: 500 per cent in forty years here, compared with only 55 per cent for the same period in Darjeeling District. So far as valley Assam is concerned much of the growth is due to immigration. Even in 1931 there was still vacant land waiting to be taken, and immigrants from East Bengal and from Nepal were still moving into the upper parts of the valley, Buddhists among them. In the extreme east of Arunachal Pradesh state the Buddhist community consists of Khamtis, a Shan-Kachin people who came across the border from Burma in the eighteenth century; in Tripura and Mizoram also, the origins of the Buddhist culture of the hill people are to be found in neighbouring Burma. So once again we find that any Buddhist tradition which can be identified as residual is almost if not entirely nil; living Buddhism here consists in some places of a Burmese tradition re-introduced into India after many centuries,

57

and in others of a Nepalese or Tibetan tradition, similarly re-introduced.

The potential for Buddhist resurgence in India

Having examined the extent of the *actual* resurgence of Buddhism in India, it is possible now to move on to consider the important subject of Buddhism's *potential* for resurgence.

Taken at face value this may not seem very great. Buddhists are a tiny fraction of the total population of India. This survey of the north-east seems to suggest that Buddhist growth in the modern period has been the result mainly of immigration, with perhaps some additional increment of numbers which the local community is able to attract from among neighbouring groups. Sometimes, as in Maharashtra, immediate social or political conditions may favour a sudden rapid growth of adherents, given that a single individual or small group is present and can communicate Buddhist values, attitudes and practices in a way that is relevant to the local mood or need. In this kind of case there are two requirements: one is the receptive local situation, and the other is the presence of a significant and effective agent of Buddhism. These need to be related to each other in just the right sort of way, for potential growth to become actual. There has to be a sufficient amount of predisposition, and Buddhism has to be seen to provide a sufficiently attractive alternative to the present condition.

A theoretical discussion of what might constitute favourable predispositions for Buddhist growth in India today would need much more space than is available in a short chapter. There may be some value, however, in mentioning two features of the contemporary situation which could be regarded as providing favourable conditions. Both are associated with the general spread of education. One is the potential which is present among those whose education has enabled them to think critically about Indian traditional society and traditional ideas. The second is a special case of the first, namely, those who have received such education and whose cultural origins are in a tribal, non-Hindu society.

Significant examples of the first kind have already been mentioned in passing: Jawaharlal Nehru and Dr B. R. Ambedkar. The first found himself disenchanted with the Hindu caste society to which he belonged by birth; the second found himself disenchanted with the Hindu caste society from which he was debarred by birth. Both, in different ways, from the position of educated, secularised intellectuals, were attracted by Buddhism. Most significantly, perhaps, one was satisfied with a personal devotion to Buddhist ideas and values without any institutional commitment; while the other committed himself to active involvement in a Buddhist community and encouraged others to do the same. These may possibly be seen as two distinct types of modern resurgent Buddhism. For Buddhism, now as always, caters for both. The existence of what may be called the 'Nehru' type will not be apparent from the data provided in Census Reports; these will provide information only concerning the second type, and may even then understate the case. The membership of the Maha Bodhi Society of India will furnish examples of the 'Nehru' type; not all those who are listed as members of the society and take part in the activities will necessarily be returned as Buddhists when it comes to Census enumeration. But that is not to say that Buddhist values are not being diffused through the agency of such people. The nature and effect of social action are not inhibited by what is entered on a Census list.

With regard to the second kind of potential for the resurgence of Buddhism it has to be admitted that this is somewhat more speculative. It may also be more specially relevant to north-eastern India. For this region is characterised by some relatively high rates of literacy among tribal peoples. Whereas the all-India average rate of literacy among scheduled tribes in 1961 was 8·5 per cent, among the Lushais of Mizoram it was more than 40 per cent, and in Manipur state it was 27 per cent.[24] With the greater ease of access to education, and especially higher education, which young people from tribal areas now have, through the attention which is being given to this by the central government and by state government, there will come the possibility of greater freedom with regard to personal beliefs and attitudes for these young people. It is true that there are conditioning factors other than education to be taken into account but education will rank fairly high in the scale of importance.

Verrier Elwin pointed out that it is not necessary to assume that as tribal people become educated they must abandon their traditional belief and become Hindu or Christian; while they are at liberty to do so if they desire, it is not an inescapable necessity. A deeper study of tribal religions, claims Elwin, 'shows that they have many elements that satisfy the heart, even though, like other religions, they have other elements which do not satisfy the mind.'[25] In a recent study by the Deputy Registrar-General of India of modernisation among tribal people the impact of education is seen to be a key factor. Among other effects (such as opening up possibilities of new occupations, associated with a Western way of life), is the new intellectual awareness it brings: 'young men and women become sceptical about tribal myths and legends and associated world-views'; this, he says, causes 'a search for new horizons'. In the wake of this experience 'some give up their religion and either become Christians or devotees of Vivekananda or some other such world teacher'. Others take to what he calls revivalism and similar movements which derive their inspiration from the past.[26] Whereas tribal people in India live mostly in areas where they form the majority of the population and are sometimes unaware of the fact that they are minorities in the wider context, the effect of education is to produce an awareness of this fact. 'By a clean sweep education displaces the tribals from their secure primitive world', and 'they begin to feel themselves an insignificant minority'.[27]

This kind of social and psychological transition is strikingly similar to the transition which was being experienced by the tribal republics who inhabited the sub-Himalayan foothills and plains at the time of Sakyamuni. The growth of large new political units of a monarchical kind into which the tribal republics or Sangha were being absorbed was producing a similar sense of loss of security and of being adrift in a strange sea where there were no moorings. The growth of an urban style of life at the cities where monarchs had their courts and capitals was effecting great changes in intellectual and moral attitudes, and new questions concerning life's meaning and destiny were being asked.[28] The movement we now call early Buddhism emerged as a way by means of which people who were caught up in such an experience could adjust to new perspectives, and could explore with confidence a universe of new horizons, while preserving in the life of the new Sangha 'of the four winds', the most valuable aspects of the old, local Sangha.

Young people from tribal backgrounds, especially those who have undergone higher education, are likely to be in a very similar situation today. Possibilities of re-orientation envisaged by Verrier Elwin and by Roy-Burman are mainly in terms of Hindu or Christian religion, or complete secularism for those young people to whom ideas about gods no longer make sense. But with regard to Hinduism as Verrier Elwin points out there are obstacles. One is the cow; to have to learn to venerate this animal is not easy for people who have never done so and are now moving into a world of thought where such a requirement seems bizarre. The other is caste: after the egalitarianism of tribal life it will be hard for a young person to accept the ritual and social inequalities of the *jati* system. With regard to Christianity also there are difficulties. They arise out of the form of Christianity which is preached by evangelical missionaries. As Verrier Elwin points out, a doctrine 'that traces the sharpest of distinctions between the convert and the "heathen", between the saved and the damned, and that insists that Christians should keep themselves apart from non-Christians, results in an essentially separatist, a xenophobic psychology, which has in many places manifested itself both in social life and politics.' It has the political effect, says Elwin, of diminishing the convert's enthusiasm for India and its culture;[29] one might almost add, of demeaning India in his eyes.

These obstacles and difficulties do not present themselves to the follower of the Buddhist way. From the earliest days both the veneration of the cow and the observance of caste inequalities have been successfully dispensed with. Neither does the Buddhist have to alienate himself from India and its culture, since Buddhism has itself contributed very significantly to that culture; nor need he feel any obligation to despise the 'pagan' culture of his own people. For, also from the earliest days, Buddhism has maintained what I have called an open frontier between the Dharma and local folk belief and practice. It is not necessary here to multiply examples of this: they are abundant in the literature dealing with Burmese, Thai and Sri Lanka Buddhism, for example. From this area Verrier Elwin quotes the case of the Sherdukpen tribe, in Arunachal Pradesh, 'who have developed an interesting synthesis of Buddhist and tribal ideas'.[30]

These considerations are offered not in any commendatory sense, but in order to make possible a fair assessment of the *potential* which exists for Buddhist resurgence in this part of India. Against these assets one will have to set the liabilities. Two, which seem to me most important, will be mentioned here, in conclusion.

The first concerns the agent by means of whom Buddhism is to be communicated. Sangharakshita records how, in Kerala, he met a man who had a deep interest in Buddhism.

Twenty years earlier, he told us, when a Malayalam translation of *The Light of Asia* had aroused the interest of many Eazhavas, he had founded a Buddhist organisation and brought a bhikkhu from Ceylon to preach the Dharma. Unfortunately, the bhikkhu had shown more concern for his own creature comforts than enthusiasm for his pastoral duties, and his demands eventually became so unreasonable that he had to be sent back to Ceylon.

Sangharakshita comments ruefully on the opportunity that was thus lost, which, if the right kind of Buddhist had been able to use, could have led to the full actualisation of what was clearly the potential for Buddhism in Kerala at that time. He adds that this was not the only case of its kind; he subsequently heard of others in different parts of India and 'eventually concluded that bhikkhus from South-East Asia often did more harm than good in the cause of Buddhism in India.'[31] Clearly it is not enough that a potential exists in the form of an intellectual interest; if it is to become a living tradition the presence of the right kind of individual or group to provide a Buddhist presence and to introduce Buddhist teaching and practice, is one essential factor.

The other liability which Buddhism has to face in India is that in neighbouring countries it has traditionally been closely associated with the state, and in more than one case has enjoyed the privileged position of being the state religion. In the cases of Burma and Sri Lanka it lost its place as the established religion of the state during the British Colonial period but soon after independence, in both countries, movements began which aimed at having it reinstated in its former favoured position. Both in Burma and Sri Lanka these movements aroused the opposition of other religious communities, and in Burma the attempt by Prime Minister U Nu to make Buddhism the state religion was a principal factor in his downfall. In the case of Thailand, the traditional role of Buddhism as the offical religion of the state has never effectively been interrupted, and today the slogan 'King, Religion and Country' indicates the way in which Buddhism is made to serve as a symbol of patriotism, and to play a supportive role for a non-democratic military government.

This association of Buddhism in South-East Asia with the state is, however, not of the essence of Buddhism; it has much more to do with the historical development of these states. In Burma, some of the opposition to the proposal for Burmese state Buddhism came from Buddhists of the Shan states, since they saw it as a vehicle of Burmese ethnic domination and a threat to the freedom and rights of ethnic minorities.[32] Heinz Bechert has cited the example of the Chittagong Hill Tracts, where communities of Buddhists have maintained their existence successfully without benefit of state patronage or political influence and without large land-owning interests of the kind the bhikkhus of Sri Lanka had.[33]

The Buddhists of Chittagong Hill Tracts and the Kachin/Shan Buddhists of northern Burma are, as it happens, neighbours to the Buddhist communities just across the borders in north-east India, and indeed it is from these Chittagonian, Kachin and Shan areas that the Buddhists of the eastern hill and valley areas of Assam, Mizoram, Tripura and parts of Arunachal Pradesh originally came. Political and security considerations now make ease of social and cultural communication across the frontiers difficult but the fact that Buddhism of this type is already present in north-east India, a type which is *not* politically ambitious and which has shown itself capable of existing without official state patronage, may be sufficient to offset any opprobrium which Buddhism might otherwise incur in India by reason of its association with the state in some countries of South-East Asia.

These, however, are only slight obstacles in the way of the successful growth of Buddhism in India. What has been considered by some observers to be a more serious fact is that there is no Buddhist social order into which educated middle-class Hindus who are attracted by Buddhist ideas and practices can transfer. How serious an objection this constitutes is open to discussion. For the objection appears to be based on the assumption that Buddhism, in order to be adopted as a way of life by modern Indians, must have the form of a culture or a social order. An alternative form, that of the sect, will be considered briefly in the final chapter. But certainly Buddhism's ability to establish itself on a large scale among the Scheduled Castes is in question, as we shall shortly see.

Meanwhile, we shall note the fact that it has been argued that

Hindu intellectuals in modern India who feel attracted to Buddhism for its rationalism, its humanism, its ethical values and its meditational practices face the problem, according to Fiske, that they 'would be in a difficult position if they formally left Hinduism'. She quotes the words of a Buddhist monk in New Delhi who said, 'Today there is need for Buddhism in India. Many upper-caste people want to become Buddhist, especially university professors and students. But only one or two do. It is hard for them to leave their social order, caste and family.' She quotes also a professor of Banaras Hindu University who regards the apparent absence from Buddhism of any 'social order' as proof that it is a philosophy and not a religion.[34] If this statement means that Buddhism has no social implications or doctrines then it must be regarded as false. But if it means that Buddhism is not normally associated with a hereditary hierarchical social order like that of Hindu caste the statement is true. That there is no system of that sort into which those who are attracted to Buddhism are required to transfer could be considered among its merits. These statements about Buddhism's 'lack' of a social order can be seen as evidence of the enduring social power of Brahmanism and the habits of mind which it encourages.

On the other hand there is a strong surge of anti-Brahmanism in India today. One of the most controversial figures of the anti-Brahman movement of the twentieth century was Dr Ambedkar. His writing, teaching and public oratory brought into being a movement which was firmly opposed to the Brahman social order. It assumed also a political character and resulted in the formation of a political party which was very closely identified with the movement, and one more to be added to the long list of India's political parties. It has also been hailed as the revival of Buddhism in India. How far it is correct to view it in this light, and whether it represents the most promising form of Buddhist revival in India today are questions to which we can now turn our attention.

Part Two

Anti-Brahmanism and neo-Buddhism

5 Anti-Brahmanism and Dr Ambedkar

The Hindu social order in the early twentieth century

In order to evaluate the work of Ambedkar and its consequences in the redesignation of some three million former Untouchables as Buddhists it is necessary to say something about the condition of that element in Indian society who are nowadays designated 'Scheduled Castes'. The term Scheduled Castes identifies the lower strata of Hindu society. Various other names have been used for these groups, such as Outcastes, Pariahs, Namasudras and so on. They were known during the period of British rule as Depressed Classes, until in 1935 the term Scheduled Castes was adopted instead. Gandhi invented for them the name *Harijan*, literally 'God's people', but many of them dislike this because of its secondary meaning, that is, 'child of the temple of God' or child of a sacred prostitute, one whose father is not known and is therefore called 'God's child'. They therefore prefer the term Untouchable, which emphasises their oppressed condition. Under the Constitution of the Republic of India drawn up in 1949 after Independence, they were made *ex-Untouchables*,[1] in the sense that Untouchability was no longer a recognised status in the new India. Strictly the word 'Untouchable' refers to the ritual pollution which stigmatises them in the eyes of orthodox caste Hindus, but the criteria of pollution vary from place to place. The practice of discrimination by certain hereditary groups against other hereditary groups on the grounds that even the touch of the latter is held by the former to be a source of pollution, is rooted in Hindu history. As André Bétaille observes: 'The links between Hinduism, the ideas of purity and pollution and the social situation of the Harijans are clear and beyond dispute. In the economically undeveloped countries of Asia, where other religions predominate, poverty and destitution may be as acute as in India, but

67

the poor—though often scorned and mistreated—are rarely regarded as untouchable.'[2] Bétaille adds that although in other places poverty and squalor result in separation from the rest of society, in India 'this separation has acquired distinctive force because of the association of squalor with defilement. Although the defilement of Untouchables did not arise simply from squalor but from a much more complex set of factors in Indian society, the material conditions of the Harijan's lives have restricted severely their attempts to escape the stigma of pollution.'[3] In Hindu society, it is clear, ritual pollution and poverty go hand in hand. But not all parts of India are equally Hindu or equally orthodox in character, hence the strength of the idea of pollution varies from one region to another.

In that part of India where Ambedkar grew up it seems to have been strong enough to make a deep impression on him from an early age. His biographer, Dhananjay Keer, describes the situation as follows:

These untouchable Hindus were denied the use of public wells, and were condemned to drink any filthy water they could find. Their children were not admitted to schools attended by the caste Hindu children. Though they worshipped the gods of the Hindus, observed the same festivals, the Hindu temples were closed to them. Barbers and washermen refused to render them service. The caste Hindus, who fondly threw sugar to ants and reared dogs and other domestic pets and welcomed persons of other religions to their houses, refused to give a drop of water to the Untouchables or to show them an iota of sympathy. The Untouchable Hindus were treated by the caste Hindus as subhumans, less than men, worse than beasts.[4]

Keer goes to say that this was not the end of their miseries. Being deprived of educational opportunities which were open to others, and of other social, religious and civil rights, they had no chance of ameliorating the poverty of their condition; their housing was inadequate and insanitary, and whereas others tilled the land as tenants, they had to live on grain given to them as village menials and to eat carrion; they were born in debt and persisted in debt.[5]

As the Abbé Dubois had observed at the beginning of the nineteenth century, the outcastes, or Pariahs, were 'looked upon as almost another race of beings, altogether outside the pale of so-ciety'.

> Throughout the whole of India the Pariahs are looked upon as slaves by other castes, and are treated with great harshness. Hardly anywhere are they allowed to cultivate the soil for their own benefit, but are obliged to hire themselves out to the other castes, who in return for a minimum wage exact the hardest tasks from them.
>
> Furthermore, their masters may beat them at pleasure, the poor wretches having no right either to complain or to obtain redress for that or any other ill-treatment their masters may impose on them.[6]

Dubois then remarks upon the fact that it never occurs to the Pariah to think that his fate is anything but irrevocable. 'Nothing will persuade him that men are all made of the same clay, or that he has the right to insist on better treatment than that which is meted out to him.'[7]

Not only do these depressed castes 'live in hopeless poverty' and 'from hand to mouth the whole year round' but they have to suffer such excessive contempt and aversion from the other castes— particularly the Brahmans, says Dubois—'that in many places their presence, or even their footprints, are considered sufficient to defile the whole neighbourhood. They are forbidden to cross a street in which Brahmans are living. Should they be so ill-advised as to do so, the latter would have the right, not to strike them themselves, because they could not do so without defile-ment or even touch them with the end of a long stick, but to order them to be severely beaten by other people.'[8]

These facts, observes Dubois, form most striking contrasts with those relating in general to Brahmans. Although even among these, he notes there are some from the north of India who are regarded with contempt by others on account of the fact that they eat fish and eggs, or even, in some cases, meat. 'Anyhow, when these degenerate Brahmans visit southern India, and their ways become known, all other Brahmans keep them at a distance and refuse to have any dealings with them'[9] While this is mild compared with the contempt with which the depressed castes are regarded, it illustrates the same point (to which he often refers) 'namely, how incapable the Hindus are of showing any moderation in their caste customs and observances.'[10]

What Dubois thus recorded cannot be regarded merely as the excessive prejudice of an early nineteenth-century foreigner. There are too many examples of such continuing discrimination against Untouchables in the twentieth century for it to be dismissed in this way.

S. Chandrasekhar, in his foreword to a recent volume on the Untouchables recalls a memory from his own boyhood. At about the age of ten, when he was travelling with his father in the Madras countryside in the heat of summer, their route crossed the wide expanse of the dry sandy bed of a river. There, at midday, they came across 'an unruly crowd of about fifty or sixty people', and saw, to their horror, 'a thin, middle-aged man being beaten and chased by the crowd from a Hindu temple on the river bank below . . . The man was an Untouchable who had committed the unforgivable crime of drawing water from the temple well [available to other Hindus but not to Untouchables] to quench his thirst on that hot day.'[11] Stories of the kind could be multiplied indefinitely, and not only from the memories of the past.

Betaille, for instance, mentions, without special emphasis but merely as an illustration, the incident which occurred on 25 December 1968 when, 'following a protracted quarrel between landowners and wage labourers, the houses along an entire Harijan street were set on fire and forty-two women and children burned to death.'[12] The Indian sociologist, G. S. Ghurye, in his *Caste, Class and Occupation*, concludes a chapter on the Scheduled Castes with several pages of summary accounts of violent action by caste Hindus against Untouchables which had occurred between 1953 and 1956.[13] M. K. Pande has recently provided an extended account of such harassment and atrocities in the 1970s.[14] Similarly, at the time of writing (1978), accounts of incidents of a similar kind could be culled from the newspapers almost daily.[15]

Such is the condition of the Scheduled Castes in India today, and such was the condition into which Bhimrao Ramji Ambedkar was born. In some respects their condition was better at that time than it had been during the many centuries previously, and than it is now; but in some respects it was worse than now. For there has been a sharpening of consciences among some Indians since Ambedkar's childhood; there has also been, however, a sharpening of opposition to what are regarded by other Indians as the presumptuous claims of the low castes.

At the time of Ambedkar's birth the Mahars, the Untouchable community of which he was a member, were allowed to serve in the Indian Army which was recruited by the British rulers. His father, Ramji, had risen to the rank of Subhedar Major in the Army and was serving at Mhow, in the western central part of India, when his son Bhimrao was born on 14 April 1891. As a Viceroy's Commissioned Officer Ramji 'had risen far beyond the average Mahar in an average Maharashtra village.'[16] This meant for young Bhimrao, as he grew up, an environment of a kind which was normally denied to Untouchables. 'Military service meant opportunities of living outside the confines of Hindu society, of educational opportunities for children of Mahar army men, of contact with the British, and experience of wide travel in India.'[17]

The young Ambedkar thus had access to both primary and high school education, an unusual privilege for an Untouchable. Even so, he was soon confronted with the fact that he bore the stigma of Untouchability. Travelling home one summer's day he and his elder brother were left to fend for themselves as their father had been unable to accompany them. Thirsty, they tried to get water, but on every occasion they were either shown some filthy water or told to go away. A few days later, driven by thirst once again, young Bhim tried taking a stealthy drink from a public supply. 'He was discovered and was beaten black and blue.'[18] Later he found that 'his hair defiled the purity of the razor of the barber who regarded even buffalo-shaving as a better and holier affair than tonsuring a human being who was his co-religionist and countryman.'[19]

His father had firmly resolved 'that his son should become a man of letters and light', and succeeded in securing his admission to Elphinstone High School in Bombay. Bhimrao succeeded at the age of sixteen in passing the Matriculation Examination. This was 'an uncommon achievement for an Untouchable' and greatly impressed a teacher at another high school in the city, a Marathi author and social reformer named Krishnaji Arjun Keluskar. He had come to know young Ambedkar, and on the occasion of his examination success presented him with a copy of his own recent book, *Life of Gautama Buddha*.[20]

From the high school Ambedkar was admitted to Elphinstone College in Bombay. When his father's funds were exhausted the Maharaja of Baroda, a reformer who had a strong concern for the education of Untouchables, granted him a scholarship to enable him to continue.[21]

During the next sixteen years from 1907, Ambedkar travelled a long way, in every sense. At the end of five years at Elphinstone College he graduated as B.A. After a few months in the service of Baroda State he was chosen as one of four students whom the Maharaja undertook to send to Columbia University, New York, for postgraduate studies. Life in New York, his biographer records, was a unique and moving experience. 'He could read, he could write, he could walk, he could bathe and he could rest with a status of equality.'[22] He obtained his M.A. degree for a thesis on 'Ancient Indian Commerce', and then the degree of Doctor of Philosophy for a dissertation on 'The National Dividend of India', which in an extended form was published eight years later in London under the title *The Evolution of Provincial Finance in British India*. During his time at Columbia University his studies had been devoted to political science, philosophy, anthropology, sociology and economics. From New York he moved in the summer of 1916 to London and was admitted to the London School of Economics and Political Science for higher doctoral work in economics. Unfortunately, however, his scholarship grant could not be renewed and he had to return to India. London University, however, had given him permission to return and resume his work within a period of not more than four years, and his intention was to work and save money in order to have enough funds to return before the end of that time. Miraculously, he managed to do so. After a bad start in the administrative service of Baroda State, where he was taunted by colleagues and subordinates with his Untouchability, and, finally was refused accommodation of any kind, he went to Bombay and was offered a vacant teaching post in the Sydenham College of Commerce and Economics. He was thus able to return to London in 1920 and resume his work there, eventually completing his thesis on 'The Problem of the Rupee' in 1922. This was published in London in 1923, with an introduction by Ambedkar's supervisor, Professor Edwin Cannan. In London he had also studied law at Grays Inn and was called to the Bar in 1922.

This brief summary of Ambedkar's academic career should serve to indicate that in his subsequent public life and intense activity on behalf of the Untouchables, and particularly in his many *contretemps* with Gandhi (who also had studied law in London) he had the consciousness of having shown that it was possible for an

Untouchable, given suitable opportunities, to achieve distinctions of a high order, equally with any Brahman with centuries of Sanskritic culture and privilege behind him. There is nothing extraordinary about such an achievement in general terms, except that in India it was, until that time, unthinkable. Many men of humble origin have achieved equal distinction, but not many Untouchables. Gandhi, when he first met Ambedkar, did not believe he was an Untouchable, but thought him to be a liberal Brahman concerned to champion the rights of the Untouchables.[23]

Anti-Brahmanism

There are two major ways which are open to the Scheduled Castes in modern India of escaping from their social and economic degradation. One is the traditional form of upward social mobility which a caste-group as a whole can undertake—that is 'by taking on the style of life and the symbols of the upper castes'.[24] This has become a stronger possibility since education in government schools has become more readily available to the low castes, namely in the post-Independence period, and also with the growth of the possibility of urban employment which has accompanied the economic development of India since Independence. In the case of a low-caste group studied by Bernard Cohn these two factors had enabled them 'to relate to aspects of the Hindu Great Tradition through reading stories available in vernacular books' and, where they have entered urban employment 'to participate in rituals derived from the Hindu Great Tradition at low-caste temples in the cities'.[25] In ways such as these a low-caste group, by educational, economic and ritual self-improvement, can lay claim to being no longer regarded as low-ranking, and can expect recognition of their enhanced status; this may possibly be given formal ratification by the Brahman purohit or pandit.

The second way of escape open to them is not to assimilate to the cultural style and values of the Brahmanical Great Tradition, but rather to reject them altogether. This can be done by affirming allegiance to some alternative cultural tradition, either the Untouchables' own, or some other of a non-Brahmanical kind. In the case of the Camars, the low-caste group studied by Cohn there was a tendency of this sort occurring alongside the cultural assimilation. It consisted in the affirming of a Camar culture-hero named Rai Das. Revered as a great saint, his life is the source of many stories telliñg of his supernatural ability. 'In many of these stories, Brahmans are held up to ridicule and are bested by Rai Das, through Rai Das's superior spiritual qualities.'[26] Cohn tells of a celebration organised by Camar college students and teachers and attended also by the Camar who had been elected as the Member of the Legislative Assembly of Uttar Pradesh State. A large procession was followed by speeches in which incidents from the life of Rai Das were recalled, and in which also emphasis was laid on the necessity for establishing the equality of all men in the new India; it was urged 'that all caste distinctions should be ended, and that the Camars, by following the example of their saint Rai Das in living a clean and saintly life, could make themselves the equals of anyone.'[27] Cohn adds that in General the stories about Rai Das have an anti-Brahman tint to them', and 'stress right action and right principles rather than the more orthodox activities of worship and ritual'.[28]

Anti-Brahmanism has been described as 'the one modern pattern of social thought which is distinctly Indian in origin and character' which has played a part in the modern remoulding of Indian society and politics; it may be regarded as basically 'the awakening of the non-Brahmans to their essential rights of human existence which caste has denied them for ages.'[29] Historically it has consisted of different movements, varying from region to region of India, many of which began during the period of the struggle for independence, that is, during the first half of the twentieth century. Anti-Brahmanism has been strong, for example, in the south, especially in Tamilnadu, where it has represented a revolt against the Sanskritic culture of the north of India in favour of the Dravidian culture of the south, as well as against socio-political domination by the Brahman caste and a movement in the direction of Tamil self-identity. In Bengal, revolt against the social and economic dominance of the Brahmans, or upper castes generally—i.e. the *bhadralok*—was widespread among the majority of East Bengal Hindus, most of whom were low caste, from the beginning of the twentieth century at least.

Anti-Brahmanism in East Bengal in the early decades of the twentieth century took the form first of all of a refusal by the Namasudras to support the Brahmans in the latters' protest against the partition of Bengal into East and West by the government of Lord Curzon in 1905. For example, in Dacca District, the Hindus at that time formed 37 per cent of the population. Of these by far the most numerous caste were the Namasudras (a Depressed Caste). Writing in 1912 B. C. Allen observed:

> Till recent years they have been regarded with great contempt by the higher Hindu castes, and as a result they have resolutely declined to take any share in the agitation against the partition of Bengal. Having been treated as pariahs and outcastes they refused to listen to the invitation of the higher caste Hindus to join in a movement directed against the established government.[30]

Similarly in Jessore District, the Brahmans, numbering only 38,000 out of a Hindu population of 668,000, had succeeded in alienating their co-religionists to the extent that the rest of the Hindus, mostly low-caste and predominantly Namasudras, made common cause with the Muslim majority of the district in 1909 to improve their social position. Protesting against their treatment by the high-caste Hindus (mainly landed proprietors) they refused to work for them as menial servants under the conditions the high-caste Hindus imposed on them and refused to cultivate their land.[31]

During the decade between 1910 and 1920 there was, comments Broomfield, 'a remarkable development in the organisation, among the lower castes in Bengal, of caste associations, which had given them a new sense of self-reliance.'[32] One of the results of this was that in the discussions which took place with the British Government on political reform in India, the President of the Bengal Namasudra Association was in a position to write to the Government of Bengal and represent to them the opposition of the Namasudras to the Montague–Chelmsford reforms on the grounds that these would have the effect of increasing the power already in the hands of the high castes. From this time onward the Depressed Classes of Bengal expressed their anti-Brahmanism in increasingly political idiom and organisation; thus, their demand for fair representation in any parliamentary system of government to be set up in the future was an embarrassment to the *bhadralok* of Bengal, for the numerical superiority of the lower castes would clearly jeopardise high-caste interests. That the Namasudras, in spite of their differences with the Muslims in certain districts, were joining forces with them in opposition to the high-caste Hindus was again apparent in 1926. A newspaper of Barisal District commented: 'From the speeches delivered in the various mass meetings held at different places either jointly by the Muhammedans and Namasudras or by the Muhammedans alone, it is apparent that the Namasudras and the Muhammedans are uniting against the upper classes.'[33] In the Bengal Legislative Assembly, which was set up in 1937 at the beginning of the last decade of British rule, Muslims and Depressed Classes together had 149 seats allotted to them,[34] whereas the high-caste Hindus could count on 58 only. By 1943 a Ministry led by a Muslim, Sir Khwaja Nazimuddin, had emerged, supported by 'a majority of the Scheduled Caste Hindus whom the Namasudra leader, J. N. Mandal, had united into a new party with the avowed object of assisting the Muslims in "undermining the foundations of vested interests and privileges".'[35]

The eventual result of this alliance of the Scheduled Castes of East Bengal with the Muslims in common opposition to the high-caste Hindus was that in 1947, the Bengali caste Hindus, faced with incorporation into a new state of Bengal in which they would no longer be dominant when India became independent, appealed for the partition of Bengal. Against the wishes of the Bengali Muslims and Scheduled Castes, this took place on 15 August 1947, the date of the British departure; West Bengal, in which caste Hindus were the majority, became part of India, and East Bengal, in which Muslims and Scheduled Castes formed a decisive majority, became East Pakistan. The wider significance of the policy of the Untouchables in East Bengal will be considered again in the last chapter.

In Maharashtra, in western India, anti-Brahmanism found early expression in the writings and the public work of Jotirao Phule. In the year 1852 he and his wife started a school for Untouchable children. It was the first of its kind in India, and it was founded in the face of insults, ridicule and severe opposition from upper-caste Hindus. In 1875 he founded the Satyashodak Samaj (Society for the Search for Truth), the general intention of which was humanistic, and against the practice of caste distinction and the denial of human rights to low-caste people. In his various writings he portrays the Brahmans as those who fleece the poorer classes, 'making them observe religious rituals'[37] throughout their lives from birth to death, at times of sickness, in *rites de passage*, in seasonal observances, and so on, and who teach that the conditions of life under the caste system are divinely ordained. Thus, 'the poor peasants at last bend, physically and economically, under the pressure of the gods and priests'.[38]

One of his works was entitled *Slavery within the Indian Empire under the Cloak of Brahmanism*. It is interesting to notice that the 'imperialists' as Phule sees it, are the Brahmans. In the interests of their imperial rule over the people of India they composed books of Hindu religious law such as the Code of Manu, in which they themselves are presented as gods on earth and the low castes are represented as demons. Apart from such mythologising, the general tone of their social legislation is conveyed in such laws as the following, taken from the Laws of Manu. Even if a Sudra is freed by his master, he is still not free, 'for this servitude is innate in him: who can take it from him?' (VIII.414). If a Brahman has intercourse with a woman of the Sudra caste he shall be fined (VIII.385). If a Sudra cohabits with a woman of the 'twice-born' castes he is to be deprived of his member, and all his property, if she was an 'unguarded' woman; he is to be deprived of his life if she was a 'guarded' woman (VIII.374). 'A Brahman may take possession of the goods of a Sudra with perfect peace of mind, for, since nothing at all belongs to this Sudra as his own, he is one whose property may be taken away by his master.' (VIII.417)

It is on the basis of laws such as these, contained in the *Manavasastra* and of the *Manusmrti*, with the religious sanction they possess, that according to Phule the Brahmans have been able to despoil the lower classes. They do so, in his view, not only because in their capacity as priests they have the monopoly of power in religion but also because the caste as a whole has the monopoly of power in the realm of knowledge and learning, and hence in their positions as government officers and administrators they are able to continue to exploit the lower castes.[39]

In the course of the development of the anti-Brahman movement in Tamilnadu similar arguments were used by E. V. Ramaswamy who in 1925 launched his Self Respect Movement. 'Anti-Brahmanism became the ideology of a powerful social, cultural and political movement for realising the Dravidian self-identity of the Tamils.'[40] The ideology of this movement centred round the charge that Hindu religion expressed the power-interests of the Brahmans, who built a religious empire on the poverty and illiteracy of the people and on their success in exploiting these disadvantages. 'He is vehement in his attack on the Brahman priests, and their constant exploitation of the people; he lists eleven occasions from birth to death in the life of every man when religious rituals demand their priestly function and for which they have to be paid "fees".'[41] This rather crude and simplistic evaluation of the place of rituals in the life of Hindus can no doubt be explained, if not excused, in terms of the controversial situation which engendered it, and the strength of the anti-priestly passions which had been aroused. A more radical analysis of this whole area of the sociology of Indian religion is still awaited.

It is possible that E. V. Ramaswamy and the anti-Brahman movement in Tamilnadu, which had begun with the forming of the Justice Party in 1916, were influenced by Phule. It is clear that Ambedkar was. In his speeches and writings after his return to India echoes of Phule were often to be heard.

Ambedkar had returned to India in 1923, when the Tamilnadu anti-Brahman movement in its organised form was only seven years old. It was not long before he began to seek ways of organising the Untouchables of Maharashtra into some kind of social and religious resistance to Brahmanism.

Ambedkar's critique of Brahmanism

In his determination to win for the Untouchable more humane and equitable treatment at the hands of their fellow men Ambedkar saw the task as something more than social reform of the kind which was concerned with such matters as rights of widows to remarry, women's rights to property and to education, the restriction of child marriage and so on. What was needed, in his view, was 'the abolition of the caste system and reconstruction of Hindu society on the basis of equality'.[42]

By this time Gandhi also had begun to express his concern for the Untouchables. But while he was prepared to fast for the sake of Hindu–Muslim unity he was not prepared to do so for the sake of the Untouchables, and, as Ambedkar emphasised among the many charges he brought against Gandhi in his book *What Congress and Gandhi have done to the Untouchables*, Gandhi was not prepared to make non-observance of Untouchability the basis of

78

Congress Party franchise, even although he had made the production of hand-spun yarn the basis.[43] Ambedkar's biographer observes that Gandhi believed in the caste system and that his aim was to keep the castes intact; it was not his purpose to refashion or reorganise Hindu society but merely to try to persuade caste Hindus to adopt a different attitude towards their Untouchable co-religionists. Gandhi 'was all the while cautious not to hurt the susceptibilities of his orthodox capitalist admirers who were the prop of his movement'.[44]

Whereas Gandhi's method was to appeal to the consciences of the caste Hindus Ambedkar's was, first, to organise the Untouchables themselves for protest and revolt. In 1924 the *Bahishkrit Hitakarini Sabha* was formed (literally, the Society for the Benefit of the Excluded Classes). Large conferences of Untouchables were held at various places in Maharashtra State.[45] A public symbolic rejection of Brahmanical Hinduism took place on 25 December 1927, when a great protest demonstration by 3000 Untouchables was held. The authority of the Hindu scriptures, with their doctrines of social inequality, were repudiated. 'The Conference declared that the *Manusmriti*, which directed molten lead to be poured into the ears of such Shudras as would read or hear the Vedas, and which decried the Shudras, stunted their growth, impaired their self respect, and perpetuated their social, economic, religious and political slavery, be publicly burnt.' This was done before a crowd of 15,000 people. 'At nine p.m. the *Manusmriti* was placed on a bier, in a specially dug pit, in front of the pandal, and was ceremoniously burnt at the hands of Untouchable hermits.'[46] •

Ambedkar's championship of the Untouchables' cause continued, both in India and in Britain, where he was a member of the three Round Table Conferences held in 1931 and 1932 in order to work out a constitution for India in accordance with the demands of the people. Gandhi was also a delegate, and there were constant attempts by Gandhi to establish himself as the true representative of the interests of the Untouchables. Gandhi was a member of the *Bania* or merchant class, and it is significant that in his book on Gandhi and the Congress Ambedkar lays emphasis on what he sees as the unholy alliance between Brahmans and Banias. W. N. Kuber summarises Ambedkar's position as follows:

According to Ambedkar, the Brahman was alien and hostile to

the Shudras and Untouchables. The Bania was the worst parasitic class known to history. In him, the vice of money-making was unredeemed by culture or conscience. He was like an undertaker who prospered when there was an epidemic. He used his money to create poverty and more poverty by lending money for unproductive purposes. The whole of poor, starving, illiterate India was mortgaged to the Bania. The Brahman enslaved the mind, and the Bania enslaved the body; between them they divided the spoils which belonged to the governing classes.[47]

In 1935 Ambedkar made clear his personal position with regard to Hindu religion in a speech at a conference attended by 10,000 Untouchables. Recalling the plight of the Untouchables in Hindu society in all spheres—economic, social, educational and political—he reminded them of the 'immense sacrifices made by them to secure the barest human rights as members of the same community under the aegis of Hinduism.'[48] He had therefore come to a personal decision. By no choice of his own he had been born a Hindu Untouchable, but—'I solemnly assure you that I will not die a Hindu,' he concluded. His declaration caused a public sensation and was widely reported throughout India.[49]

In the same year he published a booklet entitled *The Annihilation of Caste*. Caste, in his view, 'is a social system which embodies the arrogance and selfishness of a perverse section of the Hindus who were superior enough in social status to set it in fashion and who had the authority to force it on the inferiors . . . It has killed public spirit, destroyed sense of public charity and narrowed down public opinion.'[50] It is for this reason, he argues, that there have been no real social revolutions in India. 'The lower classes of Hindus have been completely disabled for direct action on account of this wretched system.'[51] Ambedkar here appeared to be moving towards the prescription of a remedy in political and economic terms. In fact, it was never produced, for, ignoring the implication of his argument, he veered off in another direction. In a speech which he made in 1938 to a conference of some 20,000 Untouchable railway workers Ambedkar declared that there were two enemies of the working class in India: these were Brahmanism and Capitalism.

By Brahmanism, [he said] I do not mean the power, privileges and interests of the Brahmans as a community. That is not the sense in which I am using the word. By Brahmanism I mean the negation of the spirit of liberty, equality and fraternity. In that sense it is rampant in all classes and is not confined to Brahmans alone though they have been its originators. The effect of Brahmanism was not confined to social rights such as inter-dining and inter-marrying. It also denied them civic rights. So omniscient is Brahmanism that it even affects the field of economic opportunities.'[52]

Let it be admitted that this was oratory, and that a man's words on such an occasion may not bear too much close scrutiny or analysis. Even so, there is an incompability between the criticism of caste in his booklet, and the priority he gives to the Brahman ideology in this speech. His booklet argues that the *social formation* known as caste has effectively prevented direct action. But in his speech of 1938 he first sets on one side 'the power, privileges and interests of the Brahman', and, dealing with Brahmanism as an *ideology*, suggests that it is this that determines social and economic realities.

In 1944, in another speech, he attributes the evils of Untouchability to caste once again; the existence of caste he attributes to Brahmanical religion, and Brahmanical religion to Brahman *political power*.[53] Thus the ultimate factor to be faced and overcome by the Untouchables is Brahmanical political power. This he regards as the real root of the social evil he is attacking and it is this that must be eradicated; any remedy short of this will be merely superficial tinkering with the situation.

Thus, throughout his various speeches and writings, of which these will serve as examples, he discerns an important relationship between economic and political realities on the one hand and religious ideology on the other. Similarly the required remedy is perceived sometimes as being political and sometimes in terms of religious ideology. Ambedkar thus appears to oscillate between the political and the religious as the ultimately significant factor, both in theory and in practice. This dualism was epitomised in the year of his death, when on the one hand he publicly became a Buddhist, and led thousands of Mahar Untouchables with him out of Hinduism into Buddhism, and on the other he was making plans for a new Republican Party, which in fact was formed, in accordance with his wishes, just after his death.[54]

Ambedkar's radical conviction that what was needed was *the abolition of the caste system* and the reconstruction of Hindu society, had, after all, remained only a conviction: he envisaged no *practical* means of achieving this revolutionary end. For the Republican Party, when it was formed, proved to be little more than 'a mere conversion of the Scheduled Caste Federation'[55] which had already served as the political platform for Untouchable communities.[56] As for Buddhism, far from having the resources to bring about the abolition of the Brahmanical caste system, it had, in past centuries, shown itself very vulnerable to the powerful opposition of Brahmans and caste Hindus. Ambedkar's one significant attempt to outlaw the caste system from India is to be seen in the way he seized the opportunity which came to him as Law Minister in Jawarharlal Nehru's government, and as chairman of the committee which drafted the Constitution of the new Independent India, which was subsequently adopted in 1949. In this Ambedkar showed his great skill and competence as a lawyer as well as his crusading spirit on behalf of the oppressed classes of India. But what constitutional lawyers could succeed in devising in committee, and in carrying through Parliament, still had somehow to be translated into social reality in the countryside of India. That need substantially still remains; what the condition of the oppressed classes of Indian society is, after thirty years *constitutional* benefit, we shall consider later. Meanwhile, there is the matter of the adoption of Buddhism by Ambedkar and some of his fellow Untouchables in 1956 to be considered. Ambedkar appears to have been convinced of the appropriateness of this decision. Certainly it was not a decision which had been reached rapidly or suddenly. For more than twenty years since 1935 he had been pondering the appropriate religious course of action to be followed once he had renounced caste Hinduism before he finally decided that the answer lay with Buddhism. How he came to this decision we must now attempt to discover.

6 Ambedkar between Marxism and Buddhism

Ambedkar: a failed Marxist?

The year Ambedkar made the much-publicised speech in which he declared his intention not to remain a Hindu was notable in another connection. In that year the Government of India Act 1935 was passed, an Act which provided for provincial autonomy and a certain measure of representative government in British India. Accordingly, the following year Ambedkar and some of his colleagues formed the Independent Labour Party, to represent Scheduled Caste interests in the forthcoming elections to the new parliamentary body.

This indicates Ambedkar's belief in the necessary interconnectedness of the religious and political realms. He seems to have acted on the assumption that these were two dimensions of the one condition suffered by the Untouchables; certainly some of his speeches indicate that he regarded the two as theoretically related. In his public analysis of the oppression under which the Untouchables lived we have noted that he frequently emphasised the inter-relation between the political and economic power of the Brahman class on the one hand and Brahmanical religious institutions on the other in a way which brought him very close to a Marxist interpretation of the Untouchables' condition. However, he was not willing to accept a Marxist prescription for changing it—that is, a prescription which would have emphasised the prior importance of political and economic action and would have relegated concern with religious ideas to a subsidiary, heuristic place at best.

His resistance to the Marxist conclusion which could well have been drawn from his undoubtedly materialist analysis seems to have been due to the general antipathy he felt for Communism as he knew it in its Indian form and as he had heard of it in its Russian form. The Communists of Maharashtra, his own state, he regarded as 'a bunch of Brahman boys'. Similarly he spoke of a

83

certain Maratha labour leader who had become a Communist as 'just a poor boy who has been misled by some Brahmans'.[1] It was characteristic of the Communist Party of India, especially in its early period, that many of its leaders were of Brahman caste. This was largely due to the fact that Brahmans were the most literate and educated section of Indian society and because, especially in the course of higher education, they were more exposed to ideas and information from Marxist sources. Moreover, as a class they, more than any, suffered under British rule a sense of political grievance. As elsewhere in colonial Asia this readily expressed itself in terms of allegiance to Lenin's doctrine concerning the interconnection between capitalism and imperialism and the appropriateness of Communism in the struggle against imperialism. But those who have been nurtured within the tradition of the caste system, especially in a superior position within it, sometimes find it difficult to throw off old manners and ways of thought. This has affected in certain important ways the character of the Communist Party in India. The strong antipathy which Ambedkar felt towards Communism was no doubt, therefore, partly due to personal inconsistencies on the part of Brahmans who had joined the Communist Party and partly to his own conviction that there were no exceptions to the rule 'once a Brahman always a Brahman'.

In the early 1930s, it has to be remembered, Marxism in India was still in its infancy, and was still strongly associated with the struggle for national independence. In 1936, the 'Dutt–Bradley thesis', set out in an article by the British Communists, R. Palme Dutt and B. F. Bradley, which argued 'that the Indian National Congress could play a role in organising an anti-imperialist people's front in India',[2] was accepted by the Indian Communist Party. This would have further alienated Ambedkar from Communism in India, since his attitude towards the nationalist movement was entirely negative, if not positively hostile. He did not take part in the movement for the political independence of India because in his view the end of British rule would mean the rise to power of precisely those Hindu upper castes by whom 'his people were always treated like lepers'.[3] The association of Communists with the anti-imperialist movement was, therefore, in his eyes merely the machination of some Brahmans who had their own elitist ends in view.

Ambedkar himself claimed that his rejection of a Marxist solution was not made on purely negative, empirical grounds, however, but on positive and serious consideration of Communist ideology. This seems to be the inference to be drawn from the statement he made in 1938 that 'the number of books he had read on Communism exceeded the number of books read by all Communist leaders [of India] put together'.[4] He was at times very critical of Communism's pre-occupation with industrial labour in the cities and its neglect of the vast problem of agricultural serfdom in the countryside. To this crucial practical issue the Communists of India paid no attention, he said, in a speech made in 1938 before a large deputation of peasants from all over Maharashtra—a deputation which he himself led to the Council Hall in Bombay.[5] Thirty years later one section, at least, of the Communist Party of India had accepted the urgency of rural problems and had begun to build a base among the peasants, rather than among intellectuals and industrial workers only. But in the 1930s the CPI, like all other Communist parties, was ideologically dominated by Moscow; moreover the period during which Ambedkar was active in India coincided with the regime of Stalin in the USSR, which ended only just before Ambedkar's death. The latter's view of Marxism was, therefore, that it was a tyrannous system which was entirely unacceptable as a way of solving the problems of India's Untouchables. In 1951, speaking at a meeting of Lucknow University students, he envisaged the possibility that the Depressed Classes of India, if their hopes of improved conditions continued to be frustrated by caste Hindus, might prefer Communism, and that, he concluded, would be a national disaster.[6] He was, however, aware of the strength of the appeal which Marxism could exert as a social analysis and as a policy for the social and economic liberation of the oppressed, and in 1953, three years before his death, he foresaw that the choice for Asia might well be *between Marxism and some alternative which would offer an equally powerful ideology and programme of action.*[7] In his view this alternative was Buddhism. He thus appears to have regarded Buddhism as an institutional religion which was free of the characteristics of other institutional religions, a view which suggests that he did not know it very well.

Ambedkar at the market of religions

In reaching his decision in favour of Buddhism Ambedkar began from the conviction that institutional religion *of some kind* is essential to human society. He affirmed this principle soon after his famous 1935 speech when he declared that he would not die a Hindu: 'Some people think that religion is not essential to society. I do not hold this view.' It was his conviction, he said, that human society required a religious foundation.[8] At various other times he made clear his view that important among a religion's functions were the promotion of social justice, and the promotion of the economic prosperity of its adherents. Every society must have *morality* as its governing principles, he believed, and this must be provided by its religion. Moreover, the *ideas* which a religion teaches should be compatible with reason and science, and should express the fundamental values of liberty, equality and fraternity. Above all, religion should never have the effect of justifying poverty.[9]

It is clear that by 'a religion' Ambedkar meant one of the generally recognised so-called 'world religions', such as Hinduism, Islam, Christianity, Sikhism, Jainism and Buddhism. All of these were present in India, and Ambedkar considered them critically, each in turn. To have decided that a *religion* of an institutionalised kind, such as these exemplify, was *essential* to human society was itself incompatible with a Marxist analysis. Ambedkar appears to have been asserting that the exploitative features of Hinduism were not a *necessary* characteristic of all institutional religion but were exhibited only in the cases of *certain* religions, Hinduism being one such. He rejected Islam on broadly the same grounds as Hinduism, for, like the latter, Islam made for social stagnation, he declared.[10] Muslim society in India, he observed, 'is affected by the same social evils' as affect Hindu society, with the addition, in the Muslim case, of the compulsory social seclusion of women in *purdah*. In his view the observance of caste distinctions was just as real among the Indian Muslims as among Hindus. Moreover, he found in Islam 'a spirit of intolerance which is unknown anywhere outside the Muslim world for its severity and its violence, and which is directed towards the suppression of all rational thinking', since the latter, he declared, was in conflict with the teachings of Islam.[11]

Islam had the further disadvantage in Ambedkar's eyes that it was of non-Indian origin. This disqualification it shared with Christianity. The latter's other major shortcoming, according to Ambedkar, was the spirit of individualism with which its Indian converts soon became imbued, and the absence of social concern—that is, of concern with Indian social realities—which they generally displayed. They were, far from acting as a force directed against caste discrimination, themselves corrupted by caste.[12]

The religion of the Sikhs, on the other hand, had the advantage in his eyes of being of Indian origin. For some time Ambedkar seems to have followed a curiously non-committal policy with a view to the possible Sikh conversion of the Untouchables. Sikhism had also the great virtue, in his view, of having a good military record. (On precisely these grounds Jainism was rejected, that is, for its strict policy of non-violence.) In 1936 plans were being made for the founding by the Sikh Mission of a college in Bombay for members of the Depressed Classes who might become Sikh converts, and there was talk that Ambedkar was to be its head. A group of thirteen of Ambedkar's followers were sent to the city of Amritsar to study the Sikh religion. However, when they took the precipitate step of embracing Sikhism they were, records Keer, 'coldly received back in Bombay, and afterwards they sank into oblivion'.[13]

At about the same time Ambedkar was showing an increasing interest in Buddhism. For example, in May 1936 at a conference of the Mahar community held near Bombay in order to explore the readiness of the Untouchables of Maharashtra for conversion to some other religion than Hinduism, he delivered a powerful speech in Marathi. He began by reminding his audience of the numerous and specific disabilities which the Depressed Classes had to suffer, and from which 'so long as they remained in the Hindu fold there was no salvation'.[14] He told them that they would have to leave the Hindu fold in order to secure true freedom. 'You have nothing to lose,' he declared, 'except your chains, and everything to gain by changing your religion.' Whether this parody of the words of the Communist Manifesto was intentional or not, the substitution of *a change of religion by the Mahars* for the *political mobilisation of the working class*, is a significant indication of Ambedkar's view of what was the appropriate mode of liberation for Mahars.

After a great deal more by way of a general critique of Hinduism he returned to the necessity for change: 'If you want to organise, consolidate and be successful in this world, change this religion. The religion that does not recognise you as human beings, or give you water to drink, or allow you to enter the temples is not worthy to be called a religion. The religion that forbids you to receive education and comes in the way of your ma-

terial advancement is not worthy of the appellation "religion".'[15]
It is worth noting that Ambedkar appears to have been unable to
accept that a *'religion'* could be the means by which economic exploitation of a Depressed Class would be justified in the eyes of
their privileged co-religionists. Rather than recognising that this
had frequently been an empirical characteristic of institutional religion—as it was, for example, in the case of the Church in Prussia
in the 1840s, the case which set Marx, as philosopher, on the track
of political and economic investigations into the structure of the
Prussian State[16]—Ambedkar concluded that such association of
'religion' and disprivilege was merely accidental and must mean
that the Hindu religion was not a 'genuine' religion, by his defini-
tion. This has the further implication that, since he ended by hint-
ing that Buddhism was the preferred alternative religion,[17] he
regarded this as an institutional religion which could *not* be
accused of permitting one class of its adherents to justify the economic exploitation of another. In fact, since he had stipulated that
the religion of his choice would be one that positively promoted
economic prosperity it appears that he was persuaded that this
would be the general social and economic effect of Buddhism. A
further twenty years were to pass before his religious preference
was publicly expressed in conversion. The intervening years were
those of the Second World War, of Britain's withdrawal from
India, and the coming into existence of the new independent Republic of India. Not until then was he able to bring his plans to
fruition.

Towards neo-Buddhism

The withdrawal of Britain from India, carried out by the post-war
Labour Government of Britain, necessitated the working out of a
Constitution for the new India. Invited by Jawaharlal Nehru,
independent India's first Prime Minister, to join the Cabinet as
Law Minister in August 1947, Ambedkar was elected chairman of
the Constitution-drafting committee a few days later. The com-
pleted Constitution was passed by India's Constituent Assembly
in November 1949, and came into force in 1950. Article 17 of the
Constitution states that:

'Untouchability' is abolished and its practice in any form is forbidden. The enforcement of any disability arising out of 'Untouchability' shall be an offence punishable in accordance with law.[18]

This was undoubtedly a great leap forward, in theory. But Constitutional theory had to be put into practice before it could benefit the Untouchables. Meanwhile, from about 1950 onwards Ambedkar's preference for Buddhism once again began to be openly exhibited. In May 1950 he visited the predominantly Buddhist country of Sri Lanka and on his arrival in Colombo told press reporters that he had come 'to observe Buddhist ceremonial and rituals, and to find out to what extent the religion of the Buddha was a live thing'.[19] In an address which he was invited to give to the delegates attending a conference of the Young Men's Buddhist Association he spoke of the rise and fall of Buddhism in India. He distinguished between Buddhism in its 'material form' which, he agreed, had disappeared from India, and Buddhism as a 'spiritual force', by which he appears to have meant something in the nature of a set of ideas; as such Buddhism had not disappeared from India, he asserted. The causes of its institutional decline he identified as: (1) Successful competition from rival popular cults, Vaisnava and Saiva, which had taken over Buddhist practices; (2) the Muslim invasion of eastern India accompanied by the massacre of some Buddhist monks and the flight of others to lands beyond the borders of India; (3) the comparative difficulty of Buddhist religious practice compared with Hindu; and (4) 'the political atmosphere in India, which had been unfavourable to the advancement of Buddhism'.[20] The last of these causes of Buddhism's decline suggested by Ambedkar, together with the fact that he envisaged its possible revival in India, might perhaps be taken to mean that he regarded the political atmosphere in India as now being more favourable to such a development. But this can hardly be what he meant, for he pointed out also that Buddhism was now found only outside India, and was therefore regarded by Hindu leaders as no longer an Indian religion; being identified with non-Indian peoples it would be all the more in disfavour politically, 'because of its extra-territorial sympathies'.[21] In fact, on this point Indian Government attitudes to Buddhism appear to have reflected very largely their political attitudes towards neighbouring Buddhist countries of South-East

Asia and the Himalayan borders. On the whole, the geo-political realities of Asia have resulted in a fairly benign Indian attitude towards Buddhism—at the official level, at least. However, in 1950 this was not yet so clear; what was a realistic note in Ambedkar's address on that occasion, as subsequent events have shown, was his warning against the vain hope that India's Scheduled Caste converts to Buddhism would be supported by the Buddhistic world outside India in their attempt to improve their lot.[22]

Four years later, in December 1954, Ambedkar attended the third Buddhist World Conference in Rangoon, and made a speech to a gathering of 10,000 Buddhists on the subject of the mission and propagation of Buddhism. He acknowledged that Burma was a leading Buddhist country but deplored the money which was squandered on decorations at Buddhist religious festivals. He suggested that the money would be much better employed in propagating Buddhism in other countries. Ambedkar's attitude towards Burmese Buddhism, and to Sri Lankan Buddhism, as it is revealed by his public speeches to Buddhists of those countries, seems to indicate that his allegiance was not so much to the traditional and often rather antiquarian forms in which Buddhism actually existed in Asia, but to a new version of Buddhism of his own conception. That he had such a 'neo-Buddhism' in view was hinted at in the course of his Rangoon speech when he referred to a book he was writing which would explain the tenets of Buddhism to the common man. This was a reference to *The Buddha and His Dhamma*, eventually published posthumously in 1957. It was at this point that he stated his intention to become a Buddhist, as soon as his book was finished.

When the nature and contents of *The Buddha and His Dhamma* are considered they appear to add weight to the idea that Ambedkar intended it as an explication of what he meant by becoming a Buddhist. For what is contained there can hardly be called a statement, in however simple language of the traditional corpus of any existing form of Buddhism, Hinayana or Mahayana. His intention, as he told newsmen on the eve of publicly becoming a Buddhist on 14 October 1956, was to 'cling to the tenets of the faith as preached by Lord Buddha himself, without involving his people in differences which had arisen on account of Hinayana and Mahayana.'[23] It was clear also that these tenets were to be given a modern expression in Ambedkar's kind of Buddhism, which 'would be a sort of neo-Buddhism, or *Navay ana*'.[24] For example, as he wrote in a letter to D. Valishinha at the end of October 1956: 'We have to consider ways and means of imparting the knowledge of Buddhism to the masses who have accepted His Dhamma [a reference to the many thousands of Mahars who had followed him in becoming Buddhist] and will accept it on my word. I am afraid *the Sangha will have to modify its out- look*; and instead of becoming recluses, bhikkhus should become, like the Christian missionaries, social workers and social prea- chers.'[25]

It was apparent, too, that Ambedkar envisaged some form of political Buddhism. In a talk broadcast from London by the BBC in May 1956 he said: 'The South-East Asians should beware of jumping into the Russian net. All that is necessary for them is *to give political form* to Buddha's teaching . . . Once it is realised that Buddhism is a social gospel, its revival would be an everlasting event.'[26] The conception of Buddhism as a social gospel was re- peated in a speech he made at the Fourth Conference of the World Fellowship of Buddhists in Kathmandu in November 1956, a month after his public conversion. He had come to the Confer- ence, he said, to declare that he had found Buddhism the greatest of the world religions because it was 'not merely a religion but a great social doctrine'.[27] Again at Kathmandu he explicitly con- trasted Buddhism with Russian Communism: referring to the latter as 'the Dictatorship in Russia', he added that 'the Buddhist system was a democratic system, whereas the Communist system was based on dictatorship'.[28] He appears to have equated the *social* connotations of Buddhism with *political* Buddhism. We shall return to this point later (see Chapter 8).

His book *The Buddha and His Dhamma* received faint praise from Buddhist reviewers in India and Burma. The *Maha Bodhi*, the journal of the Maha Bodhi Society in Calcutta, founded early in the twentieth century by a Sinhalese monk, called it a dangerous book, and commented especially on Ambedkar's claim that Buddhism was a social system; this said the reviewer, was not correct; this was a quite new orientation, and the book's title should be changed to *Ambedkar and His Dhamma*. A review in *The Light of the Dhamma*, Rangoon, struck a similar note. The author had tampered with the Buddhist texts and had accommodated them to his own views. He was a great and good man, but this was not a great and good book.[29]

It is significant that the less hostile of the two was the reviewer in Rangoon. The Burmese, particularly those Buddhist laymen who were also Burma's political leaders, appear to have had a high regard for Ambedkar. While he was in Burma in 1954 he visited Mandalay as well as Rangoon and spent a week as the guest of Dr R. L. Soni, the Director of the World Institute of Buddhist Culture. It is recorded that it was here that Ambedkar decided to make his formal adherence to Buddhism in the year 1956, which was to be celebrated as the 2500th anniversary of the Buddha's birth.[30] On the occasion of his public conversion in 1956 U Ba Swe and U Nu, two Prime Ministers of post-war Burma, sent him messages of greeting, and the latter described him, in a written tribute after his death, in very cordial terms and commented on his achievement in changing the social life of India.[31]

How much Ambedkar knew of the nature of social and economic conditions in Burma is not clear. It is possible that he may have been crucially affected by his visit to this Buddhist land which in many ways offers attractive contrasts, especially at the social level, with certain features of Indian life.[32] He may have envisaged a similar Buddhistic culture growing up in India. Whether this could ever be more than a dream is an open question. But it will be useful to examine how far Burma, as India's largest Buddhist neighbour, provides confirmation of Ambedkar's belief in the economically beneficent aspects of Buddhism and how far his own prescription for a political form of Buddhism in India would be a departure from the pattern of traditional Burmese Buddhism. To an exploration of these issues we now turn.

7 Buddhism and wealth

Indian entrepreneurs in Burma

Burma, a traditionally Buddhist country, is not, even by Indian standards, a rich country. True, Burma is rich in natural resources, but as these have remained largely undeveloped since the end of British rule Burma's reputation among the nations is not one of great commercial or industrial importance. Nor have Burmese Buddhists been notable as entrepreneurs.

In general, Indians can claim a much better record in this respect. Indeed, certain Indian groups had established themselves as a commercial community in Burma from well before the beginning of the Second World War until they were expelled by the Burmese government of General Ne Win in the early 1960s. By 1939 Indians were the owners in Burma of 7 engineering factories, 51 sawmills, 190 rice mills, 3 vegetable oil mills, 24 cotton factories and 28 other kinds of factories making sugar, metalware, matches, chemicals and so on.[1] Indian assets in terms of factory ownership in Rangoon, in 1940, amounted to the equivalent of eleven and a quarter million pounds sterling. The capital city of Burma, Rangoon, 'was essentially an Indian city', writes N. R. Chakravarti, and anyone who knew Rangoon before the mid-1960s would have no difficulty in agreeing with that description. It was 'essentially an Indian city where a very large majority of landlords were Indians, who owned practically all the multi-storied residential quarters, mercantile houses, villas, important shopping centres, theatres and cinemas.'[2] Moreover, Rangoon, although it was the largest was not the only city in Burma where India enterprise had been established. In many others—Akyab, Moulmein, Bassein, Mandalay, Pegu and Maymyo—it was Indian business men who ran most of the commercial and industrial concerns which were not in the hands of the British.

Since one of the qualities Ambedkar required of a religion was that it should promote the material prosperity of its adherents, all this commercial success on the part of Hindus, with nothing remotely comparable on the part of Burmese Buddhists, seems to suggest that he had not chosen very wisely. But it has to be remembered that it is not *qua* Hindus that Indians succeed in business. The significant differential factor is found at the level of the sub-culture, namely the caste-group or minority group to which the Indian belongs. It was not all Hindus in Burma who succeeded in building up businesses in that country; the labouring castes continued as labourers and nothing more. It was outstandingly the Chettyar caste and one or two other social subgroups of a similar kind who were economically successful. The Chettyars are a banking and business caste. In India itself the successful entrepreneurs have included also, very prominently, men of the Jain and Parsi communities.[3]

The vital question, as it relates to Ambedkar's choice, therefore, is whether in India Buddhists, as a new social sub-group would be likely to achieve economic success in tough competition with other, admittedly powerful, rivals such as Chettyars and Marwaris, Jains and Parsis. One could argue that a newly re-vitalised minority social group such as the Mahars might, given sufficiently strong motivation and favourable local conditions achieve similar economic success, as for example the Mahisyas, a traditionally agricultural caste of West Bengal, have done in the light engineering industry in Howrah city.[4] The question resolves itself into that of the *motivation* which the change to Buddhism might or might not provide for economic enterprise, and then of the favourable or otherwise nature of their local conditions.

What motivation, then, does Buddhism provide for economic enterprise? On the face of it the Burma case, in the terms in which it has just been described, might appear to suggest that the answer is none, or at best very little. Indian perceptions of the Burmese are likely to be that these are a people who, whatever other qualities they may possess do not seem to have as urgent a desire as many of the people of India have of becoming one of the world's developed nations.

Whether this is so, and if so whether it is attributable to their Buddhist culture, is an issue which has engaged the attention of a number of social scientists in the last decade or so. Their findings, which will be briefly reviewed here, will possibly have some

94

bearing on the case of the Neo-Buddhists of India. First, however, some attention needs to be given to the general relationship between cultural values and economic values.

Cultural values and economic values

The availability of material resources within any given territory (such as Burma, for example) does not entail, as a necessary consequence, that they will all be used. In any country, the particular resources that are used, and the rate at which this is done, will depend first, of course, on the *needs* of the inhabitants, or of those who control the territory, if these are not the inhabitants themselves (as in a colonial situation). What will be envisaged as the *needs* will depend on factors which can broadly be called cultural; that is, they will be in part factors derived from the physical environment, and also in part they will be cultural factors such as ideas about human nature and the nature of the world. For example, tribal peoples (such as the Chins of Burma) who believe that their well-being is secured by the offering of sacrifices of pig and fowl to the guardian spirits will regard the raising of sufficient numbers of pigs and cockerels in excess of their own domestic needs as a primary demand on time and resources. On the other hand they would not regard, say, the growing and felling of soft-wood trees which could be pulped to make large quantities of newsprint as a need, since the consumption of newsprint is not a characteristic feature of their culture. It might be desirable to grow trees for such a purpose if it was felt to be necessary in order to obtain foreign exchange resources, but this would be so only if they were persuaded that there some goods, unobtainable in the Chin Hills, the import of which the cultivators rated at least as highly as the extra labour entailed.[5]

Thus, what has *economic* value for a people are the goods (and services) they consider worth having, whether produced directly by their own labour, or obtained through trading the products of their labour. That is to say, what is worth having is determined by cultural as well as physical needs. It is evident, therefore, that the *economic* value of a commodity depends, partly at least, on *cultural* values as well as on the labour which has had to go into the production of it. *The economic structure and aims* of a society would appear to be a reflection of the relationship between a society's available material resources, its labour power and its cultural values.

Max Weber and Buddhist economic activity

We return now to the important point made by Max Weber concerning the transformation of ancient Buddhism, to which a brief reference was made in Chapter 2. The relationship between cultural and economic values is one of the central concerns of Max Weber's sociology. His work is well known so far as it concerns the Protestant ethic, but is a little less well known as far as it concerns Buddhism. The essential points of his general position with regard to Protestantism and capitalism, that cultural factors (in this case religious) can have an important function as determinants of economic activity were taken up again in his study of Hinduism and Buddhism.[6]

When Weber turned his attention to these issues in the context of Buddhist religion, the question he was mainly concerned with was whether Buddhist ideal interests have consequences in the material realm, and if so, of what kind. Weber's answer was that they did have such consequences. Cultural value was found to determine economic value in the Buddhist context also.[7] But he found that the nature of the consequences, in terms of the kind of economy which was produced, was exactly the reverse of that encouragement of capitalism which was the consequence of the Protestant ethic. The reason for this, according to Weber, lay in the essentially world-renouncing nature of Buddhism, in which 'all rational purposive activity is regarded as leading away from salvation, except, of course, the subjective activity of concentrated contemplation, which empties the soul of the passion for life and every connection with worldly interests.' There was, added Weber, 'no path leading from this only really consistent position of world-flight to any economic ethic or to any rational social ethic.'[8] 'A rational innerworldly conduct was not to be established on the basis of this philosophically distinguished, spiritualistic soteriology . . .'[9]

Early Buddhism, according to Weber, was a middle-class intellectualism: 'the rich young man was bidden unconditionally to take his leave of the world if he desired to be a perfect disciple.' Thus, the need for salvation religion does not *always* arise from 'the social condition of the disprivileged'; it can have yet another source in 'the metaphysical needs of the human mind as it is driven to reflect on ethical and religious questions, driven not by material need but by an inner compulsion to understand the world as a meaningful cosmos and to take up a position towards it.'[10]

For peasants, however, Buddhist piety was not practicable, according to Weber: 'most consistently in the salvation religion of Buddhism the peasant is religiously suspect or actually proscribed because of *ahimsa*, the absolute prohibition against taking the life of any living thing.'[11] The historical fact was, however, that Buddhism did spread into predominantly peasant societies in South-East Asia. This was possible, according to Weber, because 'the tremendous prestige traditionally enjoyed by the *shramana* (i.e., ascetics)' enabled it to exert an influence beyond the circle of the educated. 'As soon as Buddhism became a missionising popular religion, it duly transformed itself into a saviour religion based on *karma* compensation, with hopes for the world beyond guaranteed by devotional techniques, cultic and sacramental grace, and deeds of mercy.'[12]

This led to a congregational form of Buddhism, both in India and in the lands to which it spread, and this inevitably entailed an economic interest: 'the prevailing Buddhist practice was the free organization of devotees into occasional religious communities . . . The economic existence of these congregations was secured by endowments and maintained by sacrificial offerings and other gifts provided by persons with religious needs.'[13] It was thus in the interests of those who manned the popular cult which Buddhism thus became to 'endeavour to create a congregation whereby the personal following of the cult [would] assume the form of a permanent organization and become a community with fixed rights and duties.'[14]

Since the pursuit of the more demanding meditational life of the monk was beyond what was possible for the layman, whether peasant or small-town craftsman or merchant, 'the giving of alms was originally the only activity of the pious layman that really mattered.'[15] When is added to this the fact which Weber notes, that there is a tendency even in a Buddhist culture for the pious layman to regard what economic success he may have as also religious success[16] (in this case a sign of good *karma*) it will be seen that the introduction of Buddhism at the popular level is not without significant effect in the economic realm. There was one respect, however, in which Weber noted a negative effect on the economic activity of the Buddhist layman, and that was in the absence of the sense of secular vocation, or of any religious encouragement to apply oneself patiently and devotedly to the occupation which was one's allotted station in life—in other words, features which are characteristic of the Hindu caste system—for this is rejected by Buddhists. Weber had already noted that the caste ethic 'glorifies the spirit of craftsmanship and enjoins pride, not in economic earnings measured by money, nor in the miracle of rational technology as exemplified in the rational use of labour, but, rather in the personal virtuosity of the producer.'[17]

In general, however, it can be said that Weber recognised that Buddhism, in its popular form, provides positive incentives for the layman to produce an excess of goods over and above what is needed for domestic purposes in order to support and maintain and show devotion towards the Sangha, the company of monks, those who were farther advanced than the layman on the path that led to Nibbana (nirvana), a company which, nevertheless, the layman hoped one day, in some future existence, to enter.

This cultural centrality of the Sangha so far as Burma is concerned is attested by some of the earliest foreign observers of Burmese Buddhism, just before and just after the destruction of the Buddhist kingdom of Mandalay by the British in the nineteenth century. At the end of his long exposition of the life and teaching of 'Gautama the Buddha of the Burmese', the French Catholic Bishop, Bigandet, considered it necessary to add a long section, based on his own observation, concerning the community of the monks, for this was essential to the understanding of Burmese Buddhism.[18] Similarly, H. Fielding Hall, who lived in Burma from just before the events of 1885 was himself 'one of those whose army was engaged in subduing the kingdom; whose army imprisoned the king, and had killed, and were killing many, many hundred of Burmans.'[19] These words were, in fact, used by him to describe an Englishman who had died in the fighting, and whose body, floating down the Irawaddy, had been recovered and buried by Buddhist monks. Fielding Hall himself had experienced the generosity of spirit shown by the monks. 'I have had,' he wrote, 'I have still, many friends among the monkhood; I have been beholden to them for many kindnesses; I have found them always, peasants as they are, courteous and well-mannered.'[20] More than this, however, they were, in his view, the essence of Burmese Buddhism:

> The more you study the monkhood the more you see that this community is the outcome of the very heart of the people. It is part of the people, not cut off from them; it is recruited in great numbers from all sorts and conditions of men. In every village and town—nearly every man has been a monk at one time or another—it is honoured alike by all; it is kept in the straight way, not only from the inherent righteousness of its teaching, but from the determination of the people to allow no stain to rest upon what they consider as their 'great glory'. This whole monkhood is founded on freedom. It is held together not by a strong organisation, but by general consent. There is no mystery about it, there are no dark places here where the sunlight of enquiry may not come. The whole business is so simple that the very children can and do understand it. I should have expressed myself very badly if I have not made it understood how absolutely voluntary this monkhood is, held together by no everlasting vows, restrained by no rigid discipline. It is simply the free outcome of the free beliefs of the people, as much a part of them as the fruit is of the tree.[21]

Sir J. G. Scott, writing at the end of the nineteenth century under the pseudonym Shway Yoe, provides similar evidence of the central place held by the Buddhist monkhood in Burmese life. So important were the social, educational and cultural functions of the Sangha in Burma and so well were the monks esteemed 'that there are no signs,' he wrote, 'of any weakening of its strength.'[22]

What these observers of Burmese Buddhism thus emphasised—the central place held by the Sangha as a bridge between abstract, intellectual doctrines and the attitudes and values of Burmese lay people—was recognised by Weber and given full place in what he wrote concerning the importance of the congregational form in which Buddhism found social expression, and the giving of alms by the laymen as an important part of their Buddhist activity.

What Weber necessarily touched upon fairly lightly has been corroborated and filled in with greater detail in the accounts of Burmese Buddhism which have been provided more recently by anthropologists.

Recent studies of Buddhist economic activity in Burma

One of the first of these to refer specifically to Weber's account of Buddhism was David Pfanner, who undertook field research in Burma in 1959/60. This was a joint project in which similar research was undertaken in Thailand by Jasper Ingersoll. In the papers in which they reported their fieldwork they recorded their view that 'many of the issues initially raised by the work of Max Weber have particular relevance in understanding the social economics of the developing nations of South Asia.'[23]

Pfanner found that the importance of Buddhism in Burmese society made 'religious values and roles particularly relevant to the understanding of economic behaviour there'. In view of the importance of the role of the monk it was necessary to examine that role for its influence on economic behaviour. He found that 'the influence of the monk is not through direct contact or participation in economic activities or institutions, but rather in the maintenance and transmission of Buddhist value-orientations and cultural patterns which effect the economic system.'[24]

In his account of Burmese Buddhism and economic activity Pfanner shows that the two principal actors are the monk and the householder. A third, somewhat shadowy, figure is the government official, representing the secular economy. The householder has two role-relationships: first, and more important, with the monk; second, and less important, with the government official. The monk's role-relationship is confined to his relationship with the householder; he has no direct relationship with the government official and the secular economy.

This is somewhat different from the situation in Thailand, where, as Ingersoll points out, the government requests and expects from the Sangha blessing and support for its programme of community development. In Thailand, in contrast with Burma, there is a centralised, hierarchical organisation of the entire monkhood and it is therefore possible for the government to enlist its support for national purposes. It seemed to Ingersoll, writing in 1962, that 'the apparently greater commitment of the Thai clergy to development activities [would] result in a greater influence among the laity compared with the less committed monks of Burma.'[25] The assumption behind this speculation is that economic interests will take precedence over religious interests in exerting influence over lay people. This may be the case in some cultures and some countries, but it is not clearly the case in Thailand. The identification of Buddhist monks in Thailand with governmental economic development programmes has in fact had the effect of lowering the prestige of the monks in the eyes of the people, as the Thai political scientist, Somboon Suksamran, has shown in his *Political Buddhism in South-East Asia*.[26]

In Burma, even although the government (at least up to 1962) was concerned to promote and strengthen Buddhism, 'efforts have *not* been directed at encouraging the leadership or participation of the Sangha in economic development activities at the village level.'[27] As Pfanner points out, in Burma 'the monk has little direct connection with production or the means of production, with economic roles or activities.'[28] His economic significance 'is an indirect one based on the support, encouragement and transmission of Burmese cultural values and institutions'.[29] This brings us back to the fact that the major role-relationship is between the monk and the householder, and any significance for economic affairs the monk may have derives from the reciprocal religious role-relationship between him and the householder. This consists, in the layman's case, in activities which are directed towards the acquirement of merit, and in the monk's case, one might say, simply in being a monk. More explicitly, it consists in his 'observance of religious vows and precepts; in his monastic seclusion, where he studies, teaches and meditates upon the law; and in his renunciation of this world with its material goods and human passion.'[30] It is this pattern of life which constitutes what Weber recognised as the prestige traditionally enjoyed by the Buddhist monk (*Shramana*, or ascetic) which enabled Buddhism 'to exert an influence beyond the circle of the educated'.[31] Not every monk in Burma 'studies, teaches and meditates', but some do, and even in the case of these who do not the ascetic style of life which they follow represents for the Burmese layman the ideal to be achieved, if and when he can. The spoiled monk is the exception rather than the rule in Burma, and is not long tolerated (or supported) by the lay people. The important position which monks have in Burmese society, and the respect which they enjoy, has been earned over the centuries. There are no supernatural sanctions in the sense implied in priesthood. As Fielding Hall put it: 'There is no idea of priesthood about it at all, for by a priest we understand one who has received from above some power . . . one who is clothed with much authority . . . But in Buddhism there is not, these cannot be, anything of all this . . . Buddhism is a free religion. No one holds the keys of a man's salvation but himself. Buddhism never dreams that anyone can save or damn you but yourself, and so a Buddhist monk is as far away from our ideas of a priest as can be.'[32] Evidence of the same kind, sixty years later, comes from Pfanner:

> The moral superiority of monks follows from their live of blameless activity and association with the sacred literature. They are highly regarded by laymen who recognise the difficulty of attaining the knowledge and wisdom they are believed to possess, and the difficulty of leading a life so full of austerity and discipline. The difference in life-ways accounts in part for the fact that the conduct of the monk is regarded as highly admirable, worthy of emulation and thus in a sense constitutes a model of ideal behaviour.[33]

The high status afforded to monks and their teaching has two immediate effects in the economic realm, according to Pfanner. One is that certain occupations, which involve the taking of life, are regarded with disfavour; such, for example, are fishing and the raising of livestock for slaughter. Agriculture is relatively blameless since it does not normally entail the taking of life. Pfanner quotes the case, however, of groundnut crops which were being destroyed by rats. Government experts advised the use of poison for rodent control; when some farmers demurred on the grounds that this taking of life would earn demerit for them, the government announced that any demerit would accrue not to the farmer but to the government. Monks who were consulted considered the matter an affair between the farmers and the government and declined to intervene. Some however offered the opinion that the farmers' increased income from the sale of groundnuts would enable them to devote more to religious offerings and thus offset the demerit earned by the use of the rat poison. If religious merit could thus accrue to the farmer, it became a matter for the farmer to decide, and he would have to balance the effect of the good act against that of the evil.

The second indirect effect which the monks and their teaching have upon economic activity, Pfanner claims, is seen in the layman's attitude towards the accumulation of wealth. 'The accumulation of wealth as an end in itself is not admired in rural Burma, but the accumulation of wealth for purposes of merit-making is highly valued.'[34] The merit-making referred to here is mainly that of financing the initiation and ordination of young men to the monkhood (which would include also gifts for the participating monks, and the purchase of food for guests) and the annual ceremony of *Kahtein*, the offering of new robes and other necessities of life to the monks. In the area studied by Pfanner 'an average of from four to six per cent of net disposable cash income available after production costs was spent for religious purposes.' Pfanner comments on the significance of the figures, which 'may not seem to represent a large proportion of income or expenditures, but it does become significant when compared with the proportion of income saved or invested in economically advanced countries.'[35] Thus, while Burmese Buddhist culture does provide incentives for economic activity over and above what is necessary for the satisfaction of basic needs, the surplus wealth thus gained is not put to uses of a kind which will provide capital for further economic, particularly industrial, development.

A further, final aspect of the connection between cultural and economic value mentioned by Pfanner concerns the *distribution of social honour*. It is characteristic of Burmese Buddhist culture that highest social honour is given to roles associated with Buddhism.

Secular roles, such as government official, are accorded respect but generally they have not ranked as high in the status hierarchy as have religious roles, specifically that of the monk. Thus there are certain incentives or rewards adhering to religious roles (including roles such as the pagoda-builder) which do not exist to the same extent in occupational or professional secular roles. In so far as role activities functional for economic growth are not appropriately encouraged, economic growth will be delayed, for it would appear that one requirement for economic development is that certain economic roles and associated values receive reward sufficient to encourage them in the social system.[36]

There is some evidence that this is not an unintended consequence of Burmese Buddhist cultural preferences. For example, economic development, which the culture does not appear to value too highly, is in certain other ways ignored. Pfanner records that the purchase of additional consumer goods is a possibility in Lower Burma as an alternative use for increases in income, but that the preference is to devote such additional income to traditional religious, merit-making activities. In this respect Burmese Buddhists stood in marked contrast to their Thai neighbours, among whom there was 'an increasingly greater emphasis on comfort and material satisfaction sought through the consumption of commercial consumer goods.'[37] The priorities in Burmese Buddhist culture, at any rate, seem to indicate that cultural value determines economic value, rather than the reverse.

That it does so was noted by another anthropologist, Manning Nash, in his account of the fieldwork he did in two villages of Central Burma some twenty years ago.[38] Referring to Weber in general terms but without any supporting references to Weber's works, he alleges that *Buddhism*, in the economic sphere, has been held by Weber 'to inhibit economic growth, or to make believers insensitive or indifferent to economic opportunity.'[39] Weber's finding, however, as we have already noted, was that, so far as the *professional* Buddhist was concerned, there was 'no path leading from this only really consistent position of world flight to any economic ethic'—that is, of the Protestant, entrepreneurial kind. But Weber distinguished between the professional Buddhist and the pious laymen, particularly those villagers who out of respect for the *shramana*, provided him with economic support, for whom economic success was a sign of religious success, because it was the successful testing of one's good *karma*. This is, in fact, a Burmese concept as Nash himself testifies: 'It is knowledge and hard work combined with good kan [karma] that makes a favourable life and rebirth, but even these two without kan bring nothing. So the only way a man can truly test his kan (and it is religiously important to have a notion of it) is to learn from life and work hard at his tasks.'[40] Nash has here expressed, in somewhat more detail, what Weber also had noted in his *Sociology of Religion*.

Nash refers also to the work of Pfanner and Ingersoll, and in particular to their findings 'that Buddhism and economic activity are related in a way so that productive resources are spent in merit-making rather than in investment, and that the exemplary role of the monk acts against high value being placed on economic roles.'

He comments that these findings 'of course, follow Buddhist belief, but they do not get very close to the solution of the enigma' which he says Weber has bequeathed to us. This 'enigma' is identified by Nash in his assertion that 'the real central, and researchable question raised by the Weberian hypothesis' concerns 'the relations between a given religious orientation and level and type of economic activity.'[41] This is, of course, the broad concern with which the present chapter began, namely the extent to which religious and economic values determine and are determined by each other. Weber's thesis so far as Buddhism is concerned was that although at the lay, supportive level there were incentives to economic effort which Buddhist ideas supplied, nevertheless the Buddhist ethic did not encourage the growth of a capitalist economy as, in Weber's view, the Protestant ethic did. It is with the testing of this in the case of Burmese Buddhism that this chapter is concerned; the total effect of Nash's study is to confirm Weber's thesis that the Buddhist ethic discourages the development of a capitalist economy.

Nash's work certainly supports the general proposition that Buddhism can encourage economic activity and at the same time encourage the dissipation of such wealth that may be acquired as a result.

> Buddhism does not get in the way of acquiring wealth, for wealth is needed and desired for accumulating *kutho*,[42] but it does channel much of the accumulation into a form of wealth whose only future productive use is in the stream of aesthetic and religious memories and feelings it can generate. It fixes the form of accumulation so that it is not easily converted to other uses or mobile from place to place. The Buddhist emphasis on giving sacrificially, then, is both a spur to economic activity (to get the wealth to give) and a brake because it freezes wealth in the monumental rigidity of the pagodas and *kyaungs* [monasteries], or dissipates it in the feasting of *kutho* groups for both secular and religious ends.[43]

This account of the Burmese Buddhist cultural effect on economic activity has been amplified at certain points by Melford Spiro.[44] He argues that the use of surplus income for religious purposes can be explained as a disguised form of *material* interest, so far as the spenders are concerned. Faced with a choice between saving and spending, the Burmese have good reason to opt for spending. Saving is probably non-productive economically, and in any case risky. For 'the quantity of savings potentially available to the average Burman, and certainly to the average peasant would, if invested, provide him with only the smallest return, hardly sufficient to make a difference to his standard of living.'[45] Moreover, conditions in post-war Burma have been so unsettled that there has been no guarantee that the government would endure and that the savings would not be wiped out. Thus, saving would not merely mean that the peasant *deferred* such gratification as his small savings might buy him; it could well mean that he *forfeited* it altogether.

On the other hand, if he spends his small surplus in traditional religious merit-making activities, such as paying for the ordination ceremony of a monk and the accompanying social festivities, he has the satisfaction of believing that he is preparing the way, through the merit he has earned, for much better and more pleasant conditions of life for himself in the future, in some later rebirth, and as far as the present is concerned he has the immediate gratification of good food, gaiety and frivolity, and the high esteem of his friends and neighbours. It is clear that in such circumstances he will chose to spend his money, in the traditional Burmese Buddhist way, rather than save it.

Burmese Buddhist culture can thus be seen to have certain general implications for Burmese economic activity, which from the foregoing accounts can be summarised as follows. First, a certain *stimulus* to economic effort is provided by the Buddhist peasant's need to have a surplus of wealth to be used for religious purposes. But second, Buddhist culture in Burma acts as a *brake* on the personal accumulation of wealth. The factors which produce this effect are, as we have seen: first, the existence of a body of professional, full-time Buddhists (i.e. monks) who have to be economically supported by the lay people; second, the acceptance of the idea that if one cannot hope for much improvement in one's material conditions in the circumstances of the present life (true for most Burmese peasants), nevertheless he may hope for something better in some future human rebirth, if in this life he gains the necessary merit by giving liberally in general support of the monks; and, third, the practice of gaining merit by spending on special occasions, especially religious festivals, a practice which has the additional advantage of the enjoyment here and now of feasting, merry-making and earning the approval of one's neighbours.

All of this is partly specific to Burma and partly specific to Buddhism. How far these factors—both in stimulating economic effort in *getting,* and in inhibiting the accumulation of wealth through the encouragement of *spending*—would be also likely to operate in India, among converts to Buddhism from the Scheduled Castes, once Buddhism became culturally established in a specific area, is an open question. The answer is bound to be largely speculative, but there are certain data which enable some preliminary assessment to be made of the relevance or otherwise of Ambedkar's Neo-Buddhism, both with regard to the future economic condition of its adherents, and the general direction of the future development of Neo-Buddhism in India. Such assessment will also provide the opportunity for attempting to answer the questions which were raised in the first chapter.

8 Neo-Buddhism: an assessment

Buddhism and Brahmanism on the one hand, and neo-Buddhism and the Untouchables on the other, are the main issues with which this book has been concerned. Nowadays Brahmans are not what they were. Many Brahmans today are among the leaders of movements for social reconstruction, and many more are the bearers of new ideas of social equality. But the old values of Brahmanism survive and are found among less progressive, non-Brahman castes, described by an Indian newspaper recently as 'the bigots of the interior'. It is with Brahmanism in this sense that this discussion is concerned. We have explored the relationships between Brahmanism and Buddhism, and between Brahmanism and the Untouchables. Two questions have now to be considered. First, what is the nature of the relationship between the Untouchables as a whole and neo-Buddhism? Second, what is the nature of the relationship between neo-Buddhism and Buddhism, as the latter exists in India and elsewhere, at present and potentially?

Consequences for Untouchables of conversion to Buddhism

The conversion of India's Untouchables might be interpreted as being the first step in a gradual approximation of their life to something like that of the Burmese Buddhists. But if this were to affect their *economic* life, so that it came to resemble that of the Burmese Buddhists, the net result of conversion would probably not be the economic enhancement of the Untouchables' condition which Dr Ambedkar had expected. But such an outcome would depend on the development of exactly similar cultural factors among the Indian neo-Buddhists as those which inhibit the accumulation of wealth among Burma's Buddhists. Clearly, any argument concerning the probable future economic condition of

India's neo-Buddhists which was based simplistically on the assumption that the development of such factors would inevitably take place, would be fallacious. It would presuppose that 'Buddhism' signifies the same *cultural* reality in any number of different geographical and social situations. It does not, as I shall argue in the last section of this chapter.

It is clear that the present demographic, social, political and cultural environment of the neo-Buddhists of India differs considerably from that of the Buddhists of Burma. In the first place, in spite of their rapid growth since 1956, the neo-Buddhists cannot even begin to resemble the Burmese Buddhists demographically for many years, if ever. In Burma the Buddhists are the majority community and have been so for centuries. In Maharashtra the majority community are the Hindus; in 1971 they formed 81·94 per cent of the total population of Maharashtra State, whereas the Buddhists formed only 6·47 per cent.[1] No other state in India has even this percentage of neo-Buddhists. Nor is there any administrative district in Maharashtra where they amount to as much as 20 per cent of the population of the district.[2] Against such statistics supplied by the census officials has, of course, to be set the possibility there has been as been a severe under-registration of this community, and that there may in fact be more Buddhists in Maharashtra than are included in the 6·47 per cent; that is, there may be some persons who for reasons of convenience, in terms of benefits available to members of the Scheduled Castes, prefer to be registered under the latter heading. Even so, this makes no significant difference to the Buddhists' minority position in Maharashtra, since all the registered Scheduled Caste inhabitants of the state in 1971 constituted only 6 per cent of the total population.[3] Scheduled Castes and Buddhists together thus made up only 12·47 per cent of Maharashtra's population.

The neo-Buddhists are, therefore, a minority throughout Maharashtra, and even more so throughout the rest of India. What of Buddhist monks? In Burma the religious professionals, the monks, the necessity for whose economic support is a constant incentive to Burmese Buddhists to produce enough wealth in order to make available at least a small surplus, owe their position in the society and its economy to centuries of Burmese Buddhist history. No such body of monks exists in Maharashtra. A few monks have been trained, in Nagpur for example, and among the various neo-Buddhist groups the desirability of training more monks is recognised and occasionally plans are drawn up for doing so.[4] The report of a field-study of Buddhists of Maharashtra published in 1972 mentions, with reference to monks, that 'since there are so few of them', a leading person of the community is generally asked to preside at ceremonies.[5] Adele Fiske reports concerning Mysore that many people 'would like to be Buddhists but are afraid of ill treatment and have no monks'. Elsewhere she mentions the works of those monks who are to be found. These are mostly from other Buddhist communities in India and abroad: some from the Maha Bodhi Society of India; some Thai monks from Bodhgaya in Bihar; a few Tibetans who can speak Hindi; the English monk, Sangharaskshita; a visiting Sri Lankan, and about thirty or forty monks of Untouchable origin in various places.[6] Most of the non-Indian monks, representing some other Buddhist tradition, are felt by the Ambedkarite Buddhists 'to be aloof and indifferent to the needs of the Untouchables' treating them 'as Brahmans would treat them'.[7] In any case, the neo-Buddhists, like Ambadkar himself, have a strong consciousness of being Indian, and of reluctance to conform to alien cultural types of Buddhism. Even with regard to the establishment of an Indian Sangha drawn from the Scheduled Castes there has been some opposition on the grounds that this would become 'an end in itself'.[8] For these reasons, and since there is little interest among the younger men of the neo-Buddhist community in becoming monks, there appears to be a tendency to be content with lay leaders, especially if these have undergone the six-month period of training which the neo-Buddhists regard as adequate to equip a member to be a social worker or ritual specialist or missionary.[9] The venerable Sangharakshita, who was mentioned earlier,[10] contributed to the strength of the movement by teaching one-month courses for the laity on the ideas and practices of Buddhism. Sangharakshita, in various of his writings, is critical of the custom-bound conservatism and even hypocrisy of some of the 'establishment' monks of South-East Asia, and part of his role among the Indian neo-Buddhists has been to give a greater understanding of Buddhism to men and women who are living in the world the normal lives of householders.

It is clear that Dr Ambedkar also was critical of the character of the Sangha in traditionally Buddhist countries such as Burma and Sri Lanka. Reference has been made to the fact that he saw the need for a Sangha modified to meet the requirements of modern life, with monks who would be trained as social workers and missionaries.[11] This view is expressed at length in his book, *The Buddha and His Dhamma*: at the end of a section entitled 'The Bhikkhu—the Buddha's Conception of Him', containing long extracts from the Suttas,[12] Ambedkar says,

> . . . the Blessed Lord also knew that merely preaching the Dhamma to the common man would not result in the creation of that ideal society based on righteousness. An ideal must be practical and must be shown to be practicable. Then and then only people strive after it and try to realise it.
>
> To create this striving it is necessary to have a picture of a society working on the basis of the ideal and thereby proving to the common man that the ideal was not impracticable but on the other hand realisable.
>
> The Sangha is a model of a Society realising the Dhamma preached by the Blessed Lord.
>
> This is the reason why the Blessed Lord made this distinction between the Bhikkhu and the Upasaka [lay-follower]. The Bhikkhu was the torch bearer of the Buddha's ideal Society and the Upasaka was to follow the Bhikkhu as closely as he could.[13]

Then, in answer to the question, 'What is the function of the Bhikkhu?' Ambedkar replies that he has two functions—his own self-culture and the service of the people. Without the first the second is impossible. Thus, Ambedkar continues, 'A Bhikkhu leaves his home. But he does not retire from the world. He leaves home so that he may have the freedom and the opportunity to serve those who are attached to their homes but whose life is full of sorrow, misery and unhappiness and who cannot help themselves.'[14]

These quotations from Ambedkar's compendium of Buddhist teaching serve incidentally to illustrate the style of his exposition. It is characteristically Indian, in that it starts from an ancient text (in this case mostly the Pali Buddhist Suttas) and proceeds to offer a commentary on the text. The commentary frequently incorporates new ideas—that is, ideas which are not entirely derived from the text. The Ambedkarite concept of the monk and his role differs considerably from that found in the traditional Buddhist countries of South-East Asia. In Burma, for example, emphasis on teaching is limited largely to the traditional role of (some) monks as village schoolmasters. Apart from that there appears to be some mild resistance to the idea of devoting time to teaching lay people, as Melford Spiro has recorded.[15] 'That is not our concern. Our concern is to seek *nibbana*', was the characteristic monkish comment he received in upper Burma. If Ambedkar's requirement—that monks should become social workers and missionary teachers—were adopted in Burma it seems fairly clear from Spiro's evidence that the number of Burmese men wishing to become monks would be seriously reduced.

In any case, monks are not nearly so prominent a feature of the Buddhist scene in Maharashtra and neighbouring states of India as they are in Burma and other South-East Asian countries. Nor are they likely in the foreseeable future to become so.

Another element in the Burmese cultural situation which acts as an incentive both to *get* wealth, and also to *spend* it on the Sangha is the idea that the layman will, in doing so, improve his material condition in some future human rebirth. Such an idea is ruled out by Ambedkar's interpretation of Buddhist teaching. In Ambedkar's view the belief that good or bad actions (karma) in one life affect the condition of the doer of those actions in some future human existence was not an element of the Buddha's teaching, for among the principal ideas which were *rejected* by the Buddha, according to Ambedkar, were: belief in *the soul (atman)*; belief in the *transmigration* of the *soul*; and belief in *karma* as the determining of a man's position in one life by deeds done by him in a previous life.[16] Instead of the doctrine of the transmigration of the soul the Buddha taught 'the doctrine of re-birth'.[17] This Ambedkar explained as follows, using a familiar simile from the Buddhist texts:

> There is no contradiction. There can be rebirth even though there is no soul.
> There is a mango stone. The stone gives rise to a mango tree. The mango tree produces mangoes. Here is the rebirth of a mango.[18]

Ambedkar's emphasis on the rejection of the idea of the soul by anyone who would correctly understand Buddhist teaching is in keeping with the central emphasis of Buddhism in its classical forms. Together with this it is necessary also to have insight into the *conditionality* of all existence (*paticcasamuppada*).[19] One who has

such insight, it is said, 'everywhere, in all the forms of existence
. . . is beholding merely mental and physical phenomena kept
going by their being bound up through causes and effects'.[20] In
other words, 'No doer of the deed is found; no one who ever reaps
their fruits; empty phenomena roll on: this view alone is right and
true,' as the classical compendium of the Pali Buddhist thought,
the *Visuddhimagga*, puts it.[21]

The popular idea that an individual will *himself* experience a
'better' existence at some later stage of history which, as we have
noted, is found among Burmese Buddhist laymen thus owed more
to the *Hindu* doctrine of the transmigration of the soul than to
authentic *Buddhist* teaching. Ambedkar was at this point well
within the received Buddhist tradition; in so far as he was responsible for innovation, it was in other directions than this. For him it
was important to expose the exploitative potential within the
Brahmanical doctrine that he who had done good deeds would
have a rebirth in the womb of a Brahman, Ksatriya or Vaisya
woman (that is, as a caste Hindu), whereas he who had done bad
deeds would have a rebirth in the womb of a Sudra woman. For
this well-known Brahmanical formula has the obvious application, that he who is born of Sudra caste must have done bad
deeds formerly, while caste Hindus must have done good deeds to
merit such favourable transmigration of their souls. In
Ambedkar's words, 'The law of karma as formulated by the Brahmans, thought the Buddha, was calculated to sap the spirit of
revolt completely'—that is, of revolt against acceptance of oppression by others on the grounds that one's transmigrated soul
was receiving the due rewards of previous bad actions.[22]

To return to the question of the possible cultural assimilation of
neo-Buddhism in India to that of Burma it becomes evident that
on two major points Ambedkar's neo-Buddhism constitutes, in
certain respects, a critique of the Burmese variety. On one point in
particular—the nature and function of the Sangha—his critique is
explicit, and on the other—the idea of *personal* rebirth—it is
implicit.

Thus the major factors which in the Burmese case serve to *encourage* economic activity of a certain kind (that is, a certain accumulation of wealth, followed by its expenditure in the pursuit of
aims which rely on the idea of personal re-birth) are not likely to
develop in the context of India's neo-Buddhism. Since in the case
of the latter monks are few, and large amounts do not have to be

contributed to their upkeep, and since the kind of expenditure which is understood in Burma as an investment in a good 'transmigration' is in neo-Buddhism relegated to the realm of Brahmanically influenced notions, the incentives to wealth-accumulation which govern the economic activity of Burma's Buddhists will not be found among Indian neo-Buddhists.

This, however, does *not* mean that India's new Buddhists will not experience economic enhancement of their condition as a result of their conversion; only that such modest wealth as they may accumulate will not be dissipated in the Burmese manner. Nor is it so likely to be dissipated in the manner notorious in traditional Hindu India, that is, on wedding ceremonies and the attendant festivities.

In India this constitutes one of the most notorious causes of indebtedness and poverty. Other traditional Hindu ceremonies which involve the villager in great expense are those associated with birth and death. A recent survey concludes that even today these religious practices and customs still have a profound effect on the lives of the villagers, for they entail great expenditure as a result of which the villager lives permanently under a weight of debt. In the case of marriage, for example, apart from the cost of the lavish hospitality and general pomp and show, bride-price (where this is applicable, as it is among the Mahars) 'can cost anything between two thousand and eight thousand rupees. Money for this has to be borrowed from the money-lender at a high rate of interest.'[23] In the case of Hindu customs associated with birth and death 'each villager borrows at least five hundred rupees'. In many cases this will be considerably more than the household's total income for one year. A survey of villages of eastern India between the years 1956 and 1967 shows that in rural West Bengal, Orissa and Bihar more than half the households in the villages surveyed were heavily in debt, the amounts involved for each household totalling at least a year's income and in many cases considerably more. In two-thirds of the cases of indebtedness the money had been borrowed to meet consumption expenses of the traditional kind, rather than for the purpose of improving agricultural production.[24]

Conversion to Buddhism has, for the Mahars, meant a change in this respect. T. S. Wilkinson, reporting on field work carried out in Maharashtra in 1963, provides some details of the changes in Mahar social and ritual practices. 'The marriage ceremony has

114

been very much simplified with reference to time, money and rituals . . . Before conversion it was also customary for the bridegroom's party to make some cash payment to the bride's party before the solemnisation of marriage. This practice is now frowned upon and one who does it is penalised.'[25] 'The marriage dinner is also a simple affair and no non-vegetarian dishes or alcoholic drinks are served.' He adds that the latter, in particular, which formerly was always regarded as essential was not only the cause of quarrels and disorderliness but also added very greatly to the expenses, since a wedding without alcohol would be boycotted. Large amounts of money had therefore to be borrowed, in order to provide what was expected in the way of food, drink and gifts or ornaments and clothes. Among the Buddhist Mahars 'all this is now condemned and no public drinking is in evidence at wedding receptions or dinners.'[26] An incidental effect of the abandonment of alcoholic drinks has been a lessening of inter-personal tensions as well as an improvement of economic condition of the family as a whole.[27]

Another effect of conversion noted by Wilkinson is the new attitude towards education, taking the form of a much greater desire than formerly on the part of parents that their children should attend school and college, even although they themselves in most cases have received little or no formal education.[28] This is likely to have the effect of improving the economic position of these who receive such higher education; the most probable avenue of advancement is in government service, however, rather than in industry or commerce. Entry into the public service is much easier for them because of the system of reservation of a certain percentage of government posts for Untouchables. The type of education open to Untouchables does not fit them for careers in industry or other professions and there is in any case a bias against the entry of Untouchables into non-government employment.[29] Thus only the tiniest trickle of educated Untouchables is at present able to find its way into the business and professional world. As far as private commercial firms are concerned, in India these are, notoriously, networks of family, caste and regional connections. The few Untouchables who have managed to enter the business world have done so, according to Harold Isaacs, by concealing their identity.[30] Until social attitudes in India change it is unlikely that the way will be open to Untouchables' success in the world of private enterprise. Their hope would therefore appear to lie in some much greater measure of real social and political change then has so far taken place in independent India.

In spite of such persisting discrimination on the part of caste Hindus, however, an important effect of conversion to Buddhism on the Untouchables themselves is the new sense of personal dignity which they feel. Adele Fiske, on the basis of personal observation and interviews notes that, whatever their occupation, the new Buddhists 'all repeat one motif, that to be Buddhist means to them to have become a human being, no longer to feel Untouchable, degraded, polluting, but to have hope and human dignity for themselves and for their children.'[31] Eleanor Zelliott mentions the effect of conversion to Buddhism having been the removal of a sense of inferiority, a sudden sense of release, a psychological freedom, a new spirit of self-confidence which was noticeable to others, a sense of progress and of change from Hinduism.[32] One of Ambedkar's followers, who has himself benefited from the education in the first college established by the People's Education Society, founded by Ambedkar, has written of the new dignity, self-respect and self-reliance which Ambedkar instilled into the neo-Buddhists.[33]

The conclusion to be drawn from these various accounts of the neo-Buddhists is that their conversion to Buddhism has resulted in some limited improvement in their economic and social circumstances, in spite of the many adverse factors which still dog their progress. So far, however, this improvement has been experienced by a relatively small proportion of India's Untouchables: some three million out of seventy million. The effect has been confined mostly to the Mahar community of Maharashtra state, and the Jatavs of Uttar Pradesh. Why this has been so is fairly clear; it can be accounted for in terms of Ambedkar's personal role.

The role of Ambedkar as culture-hero

Neo-Buddhism is one facet of the movement begun by Dr Ambedkar. The other is political. They combine in one cult, that of Ambedkar as culture-hero; in Weberian terms, as exemplary prophet.

The *exemplary* prophet is a type which can be recognised in contrast with that of the *ethical* prophet. The latter, according to

Weber, is 'an instrument for the proclamation of a god and his will'; he preaches a message which he has received from the god and 'demands obedience as an ethical duty'. The contrasted type is 'an exemplary man who, by his personal example, demonstrates to others the way to religious salvation, as in the case of the Buddha. The preaching of this type of prophet says nothing about a divine mission or an ethical duty of obedience, but rather directs itself to the self-interest of those who crave salvation, recommending to them the same path as he himself traversed.'[34]

This description fits very well with the exemplary role in which Ambedkar is seen by his Mahar and Jatav followers. By his own Scheduled Caste community, the Mahars, he is seen as the ideal type of the Untouchable who, against overwhelming odds, succeeded not only in gaining school and college education but also in being awarded higher doctorates from foreign universities, in New York and London. His unrelenting, lifelong devotion to the cause of his people's liberation from the oppression which they suffered under the caste system, expressed in his fearless public political activity on their behalf, his attacks on the evils of Brahmanism and his public renunciation of the Hindu religion and adherence to the Buddhist way, constitutes for the Mahars not only a source of inspiration but also an example which they themselves can follow. It was a pattern which he had *recommended*, but had not insisted they should follow.

That Ambedkar should have been accepted as a culture hero by the Jatavs, an urban Scheduled Caste community of Agra, is less easy to understand. Agra is five hundred miles from the border of Maharashtra, and is not only in a different state (Uttar Pradesh) but also in a different language region (Hindi, rather than Marathi). Owen Lynch has provided extensive studies of the connection between Ambedkar and the Jatav caste.[35] In answer to the question of how this man, a 'foreigner' in Jatav terms, could gain a hold over the minds and hearts of the Jatavs, of a kind moreover which borders on worship, Lynch identifies four socio-cultural components of Ambedkar's charisma: these are (1) cultural, (2) historical, (3) structural and (4) symbolic.[36]

The cultural component is the religious–heroic tradition found among the Jatavs, and exemplified most clearly, in an earlier period, in their veneration of Kabir the sixteenth century north Indian saint who taught that all men, Hindu or Muslim, are brothers, and who rejected the caste system and preached that salvation was to be achieved by faith and devotion to God. Into this cultural tradition of religious reform Ambedkar clearly fitted very well; his teaching, says Lynch, struck sympathetic vibrations with those of Kabir.[37]

The historical component of Ambedkar's charisma is found in the actual personal relations he had with the Jatavs. When Gandhi at the Round Table Conference in London (1930/31) claimed to be the true leader of the Untouchables of India, the Jatavs of Agra sent a telegram to London supporting Ambedkar as their leader and the rightful representative of their views; they had already recognised the similarities between the Mahars' position and their own and had identified their two causes as one. Later, Ambedkar visited Agra in 1946 and 1956 and made public speeches to large audiences of the Scheduled Castes of that city, in one case amounting to a crowd of a hundred thousand people packed together in a great open space.[38] He was, thus, known by sight to the vast majority of the Jatavs of Agra, who had also experienced his charisma.

The structural component was provided by Ambedkar's place in Indian society: he was an Untouchable, one who could understand the problems and feelings of other Untouchables; but he was also the occupant of positions of great prestige in India, as barrister, constitution-maker and cabinet minister; and he was recognised by the Jatavs as a revolutionary—that is, in the sense of being the most outstanding leader and advocate of an anti-caste, social revolution in India, and in this respect was identified with them, who also were commonly regarded in Agra as revolutionary troublemakers.[39]

The symbolic component of Ambedkar's appeal consists in the fact that for the Jatavs he is one in whose achievements they can find vicarious satisfaction, and in whom they have an exemplar. His symbolic role is already apparent in 'the many poems and ballads which Jatavs now sing about Ambedkar'.[40] Lynch concludes that Ambedkar has become an integral part of the neo-Buddhist myth whose prophet he was.

This, too, is an important aspect of neo-Buddhism. The word 'myth' is being used here in the sense developed by Edmund Leach, that is, as having 'dynamic and motivational power for social change', as providing 'not just models *of* reality but also models for reality'.[41] A myth in this sense was provided for the Mahars by Ambedkar in his re-interpretation of the history of

Indian Buddhism and the history of the Untouchables. This is contained mainly in his book *The Untouchables: Who Were They and Why They Became Untouchables*, published in 1948, and to some extent in *The Buddha and His Dhamma*. The main argument of the former book is that the Untouchables of today are the descendents of the Buddhists of ancient India, men who suffered from the hostility of the Brahmans, and were forced out to the periphery of Hindu society, where, because of the desperate nature of their circumstances, they had to take to eating the carcases of cows, and thus became polluted outcastes. The myth purports to explain the social reality of the Untouchables' present condition and, what is more, presents them as the true indigenous people of India, the Kshatriya class, displaced by Brahman invaders whose alien culture had been forced upon the original inhabitants.

The myth also provides a model *for* reality in that it implies that these are past wrongs which now have to be righted—the Untouchables must recover their Buddhist heritage, throw off the alien traditions of Brahmanism and take their place once again as the real Kshatriya class, the rightful owners of the land.

It is of this myth, or message, that Ambedkar is the *exemplary prophet*. His life demonstrates the struggle against the oppression associated with Brahmanical tradition, and the recovery of human rights and dignity by the oppressed ancient people. He represents the ending of their long silence and suffering, for he himself inaugurated the new era. The way is now open for others, in increasing numbers, to follow. This, at least, is the light in which Ambedkar is seen by the Mahars. Another way of expressing this would be to say that he has provided for the Mahars and, indirectly, for the Jatavs, a way of affirming their identity, *with pride*.

But this identity requires identification with Ambedkar, either as a Mahar, or, in the case of the Jatavs, as one of a group which has cultural, historical, structural and symbolic affinities with him. Not all Scheduled Castes have such affinities. Not all share even some kind of a religious–heroic tradition; not all had actual personal relations with Ambedkar, and while many might feel the appeal of the structural component in his charisma, not all share even in a mild degree the identity of revolutionaries. For many Scheduled Castes, therefore, he has no symbolic role, and the myth of which he is the exemplary prophet fails in those cases to find any response. In other words, not all Scheduled Castes have been attracted to neo-Buddhism; its appeal has been of restricted scope.

Political disenchantment and diverging paths

There is another aspect to the limited success of the movement inaugurated by Ambedkar; this is seen in the realm of party politics. The party founded by Ambedkar in 1936,[42] the Independent Labour Party, had been re-organised in 1942 as the Scheduled Castes Federation. This had a further successor in 1956 in the Republican Party. Ambedkar announced the formation of a new party, which was to represent the interests of *all* dispossessed classes, at about the same time as his public conversion to Buddhism, in the autumn of 1956, a month or so before his death.[43] To many of his political associates the formation of a party which would act on behalf of all Scheduled Castes and Scheduled Tribes was the important event. Ambedkar's conversion, and that of the Mahars to Buddhism, was regarded as a political mistake by some of these associates.[44] But for Ambedkar the two events seem to have had a *necessary* connection. It will be recalled that he had advocated a political Buddhism[45] as the need for Asia in the twentieth century; it is possible that it was in this light that he conceived the role of the Republican Party.

Certainly it has been closely identified with the neo-Buddhists from its inception. In Maharashtra, at least, comments Zelliott, 'Republican Party members are Buddhists; Buddhists are Republicans. The number of Congress Buddhists can be counted on the fingers of one hand. Ostensibly, the leaders of the Republican Party are the leaders of the Buddhist movement.'[46] It may be doubted whether this close interconnection between the Republican Party and the neo-Buddhists has benefited either of them. That it exists at all betokens mainly the posthumous power of Ambedkar's charisma upon his followers, rather than Ambedkar's political wisdom or foresight. It is true that these were the two fronts, as it seemed to him, on which he had been fighting throughout his public life: the religious and the political. The Hindu social order he had rejected by becoming a Buddhist. The Indian National Congress he had rejected by his leadership of the Scheduled Castes Federation. The latter was now, in its new form, to be the political instrument for *all* the dispossessed, Scheduled Castes and Scheduled Tribes most notably; all those whom, it seemed to Ambedkar in the disappointments of his last years, Congress had only betrayed. Thus, neo-Buddhism and the Republican Party were to be the complementary agencies to save India from that extreme violent protest which might soon well up from the despair of India's oppressed classes. The ultimate threat, as he saw it in the 1950s, was Communism, and in the 1950s that could mean only Soviet Communism. In this dangerous direction he believed the disprivileged might turn in desperation, in the face of Hindu social intransigence and Congress's political dissembling. If they did, it would result in their coming under a tyranny even heavier than that of caste. This appears to have been the direction of his thought in the last year or so before his death.[47] But Buddhism, he believed, could provide a genuinely humanist ideology in place of the false humanism of the Soviets; and the Republican Party would, he hoped, become the instrument for the achievement of a genuinely democratic socialism. The latter had now become a possibility in the new political conditions existing in independent India, and in his view this was the form of social organisation appropriate to a Buddhist culture.[48] It could not be achieved, in Ambedkar's view, through the agency of Congress, for this was not a genuinely democratic force.[49] Thus Buddhism and the Republican Party together were to be the effective means for achieving that humanistic and democratic social order, which it would be folly to expect from either Communism or Congress.

The Republican Party has failed to meet these expectations. It failed to attract more than a minority of the dispossessed classes. Apart from the Mahar and Jatav castes, who are its main supporters, other Scheduled Castes and Tribes have given their political support in a variety of other directions—whether to Congress, or to the Communist Party (Marxist), or to tribal or regional parties such as the Jharkhand Party of Chota Nagpur. Even where Untouchables have been members of the Republican Party, they have not always supported their candidate when the time came to vote, on the grounds that he would have little prospect of winning and a vote for him was a vote wasted.[50] In general, Scheduled Caste leaders have tended to support the dominant party in their region.[51] The Republican Party has not had complete support from neo-Buddhists. Some of the leaders of the Buddhist Untouchables in Nagpur have criticised the Party's leaders and their policies on various grounds, including their political ineffectiveness.[52]

121

Not surprisingly, therefore, Ambedkar's 'political Buddhism' was already being quietly revised by some Buddhists within ten years of his death. The revision was of a kind which would make the movement more specifically *religious*. Those responsible for this revision are leaders who stand consciously apart from politics: 'the writers of the dozens of pamphlets on Buddhist ceremonies and doctrine, the pilgrims to Bodhgaya and Sarnath, the young men who learn enough Pali to lead *wandana* (prayer) and conduct wedding, naming and funeral ceremonies, the thinkers, the worriers' whose effort is directed towards creating 'a new religious culture that is unrelated to the political field'.[53]

On the other hand, there is a small section of the movement which can be regarded as the heir to the strongly *political* emphasis which characterised Ambadkar's lifelong public activity, but which now sees the proper expression of such political concern in terms of Communism. Zelliott noted that the 'Buddhists themselves often say that except for Dr Ambedkar, who was always critical of the Communist Party, and for the Buddhist conversion, the Mahars would be Communists.'[54] In Agra City Lynch also found that some Buddhist leaders were conscious of this as a possibility which was still open, and expressed it to him in such statements as the following: 'If at the time reservations end, the Republican Party has died, then all will turn to Communism. Where else is there any hope of fighting and an organisation to do it?' and 'If the Party dies, then there is only Communism. Communism is where all people are equal.'[55]

Such a possible development, of which there are still very few actual signs, would in any case not find favour with the religious wing. It seems clear that for the Mahars and Jatavs there are two alternative, divergent paths ahead, and for most of the other Scheduled Castes of India one of these, the Buddhist path, is unlikely to be given a second thought. As a road to the resolution of their conflict or as a way out of their oppressed condition, in the context of a predominantly Hindu India Buddhism would appear to them to be a dead-end. Whatever movement or ideology captures the allegiance of the majority of the Scheduled Castes it is unlikely now to be neo-Buddhism. It is significant that, as Kuber points out, the process of conversion of the Scheduled Castes almost came to an end within a short time after Ambedkar's death; this is an indication that it was seen to be inadequate and ineffective as a means of remedying their social condition.[56] The Scheduled

Tribes, moreover, already have other models of modernisation and social progress before them, and in general they are not likely to be so impressed as was Ambedkar by the fact that Buddhism had *Indian* origins.[57] Nevertheless, as we noted in Chapter 4, there are reasons for supposing that Buddhism might appeal to some younger people from tribal backgrounds.

The continuing depressed condition of the Scheduled Castes

In the matter of the choice between the neo-Buddhist path and political mobilisation on a wider base two points for comment remain.

The first is that the case of the Scheduled Castes of East Bengal in the three decades before the Second World War has some relevance to what has happened in India since then. The East Bengal case was touched upon in Chapter 5. What is noteworthy in that connection is that the success achieved by the Scheduled Castes when they formed a common political front consisted not only in the fact that they gained a new sense of self-reliance themselves, but that they acted in cooperation with Muslims in East Bengal, and thus by united action undermined the dominance of the caste Hindus. But the latter is not the proper term in this context; it is important to notice that in this case the line of division was socio-economic rather than one of religion or caste. The division was between mainly Muslim and Scheduled Caste *peasants* and small town traders, etc., and mainly caste Hindu *landowners*. The Republican Party of India, on the other hand has not succeeded in providing a common front for all disprivileged groups along socio-economic lines, although it has occasionally made common political cause with Muslims on certain issues.[58] In India, however, there are greater problems than there were in East Bengal; 'stable intercaste alliances based on common class interests are extremely difficult to effect under Untouchable leadership', comments Dushkin.[59]

The second point to be noted is that some observers have suggested that there is no further need for political action on the part of the Scheduled Castes, since their social condition is now improving noticeably, albeit fairly slowly. 'All that is needed fundamentally has been provided in the Constitution of India,' runs the argument of such observers; in the course of time the progress

123

which has already been made in implementing the Constitution will lead to the removal of the 'handicaps' from which the Scheduled Castes suffer. An example of this view of things is the optimistic conclusion reached by Santokh Singh Anant in 1971 at the end of his report on a survey of inter-caste attitudes in Agra, Delhi and Varanasi which had been carried out in 1968. The responses of 168 individuals of the Scheduled Castes, 86 of whom were urban and 82 rural, were examined. To questions concerning physical contact with higher castes, entry into temples, use of wells and water-taps, and opportunities of employment, changes for the better were reported by a significant percentage of the respondents; in most cases at least 50 per cent of respondents reported major changes of attitude on the part of caste Hindus. All this is said by the writer of the report to 'indicate a much better situation than predicted by an eminent Indian social scientist' [M. N. Srinivas], who had taken a more sceptical view and had asked for a nationwide survey. The report then goes on to quote the *earlier* (1965) opinion of M. N. Srinivas (in conjunction with André Bétaille) that 'the caste concept in India is weakening, and the social system is becoming more fluid and the gulf that has separated the Harijans from the rest of society is inexorably narrowing.'[60]

André Bétaille, however, has more recently (1972) argued that basic to the condition of the Untouchables in India is their *poverty*. The 'pollution' which in the view of caste Hindus these low castes carry is directly related to this by Bétaille: 'material deprivation and ritual impurity reinforce one another. The poor are unclean, both physically and ritually. The very squalor in which the majority of Harijans live stands in the way of their establishing a new social identity.' His final conclusion is that 'the material conditions of the Harijans' lives have restricted severely their attempts to escape the stigma of pollution.'[61]

From Uttar Pradesh comes a report on a wider-ranging survey than the one just mentioned which was based on Agra, Delhi and Varanasi.[62] Appended to this largely statistical analysis of the socio-economic characteristics of the Scheduled Castes population of Uttar Pradesh is a long list of atrocities on members of these castes committed in one year alone (1973), and reported in the press. Even this list tells only a small part of the story, since rural news coverage in the press in this state is very thin. The writer of the report notes 'that all sorts of cruelty and violence have been done to the Harijans on all kinds of pretexts, some of them very trivial.'[63] The problem is more acute in the western part of the state, he adds, where it is rooted in the system of agrarian relationships.[64] In conclusion he notes that while 'Harijans are still living in a society where they could be stoned, or burnt, or hacked to death on disputes arising over the use of the most elementary human rights' the problem is still being viewed 'with a characteristic naïveté' and solutions are still being sought which depend on gullibility.[65] A recent analysis of the situation in Kerala similarly emphasises the persistence of the oppressed condition of the Scheduled Castes in that state. 'The policies followed by the government for the uplift of the Harijans have not had any perceptible economic impact on those sections for whom they are primarily meant. Glaring disparities are seen in the size and pattern of landholding, employment opportunity, income level and educational attainment between Harijans and the rest of Kerala society.'[66]

Bland reliance upon the implementing of the provisions of the Constitution by the ruling Congress Party, dominant in India until 1977, does not seem to have been proved right in this respect. But his hopes have been proved false by the failure of the disprivileged sections of Indian society to engage in *united* political action on their own behalf. That Ambedkar's policy of linking a political party with the neo-Buddhist movement was partly responsible for prejudicing the issue and alienating the majority of the Scheduled Castes from the political base which the Republican Party might conceivably have provided can hardly be doubted. In doing this he may also on the other hand have prejudiced the prospects of any new Buddhist movement arising in India.

In the context of the Indian social situation the vast majority of the Scheduled Castes, in failing to respond to Ambedkar's invitation to follow him into Buddhism have, whether consciously or not, made a realistic decision. The dominant class and the dominant values in India today are Hindu, notwithstanding the secular ideals of the Constitution. For although in demographic terms the dominance of Hindus is not overwhelming, they constitute the largest single community, whereas the rest, the minority communities, are a disparate collection with little in common but their minority status. The Scheduled Castes are in an ambiguous position. Socially they are not accepted as forming one community with other Hindus, either in normal social communication or in educational, political and economic terms. Even in the pre-dominantly Hinduistic society of modern India attitudes towards the status of Brahmans, however, are ambivalent. In certain respects Brahmans suffer from discrimination against them in some areas of India, especially in the south, where it arises by reaction from the privileged position they held for so long, as we noted in Chapter 6. But the social attitudes which other strata of Indian society have learnt from Brahmans persist, so that although most of the socially innovative, emancipated and liberal individuals nowadays are as likely to be of Brahman caste as any other, the old attitudes appropriate to Brahman social dominance are still found among other less progressive sections of Indian society. The values and norms of what may be called classical Brahmanism have not changed; it is merely that, having been inherited by other classes, they have shifted their social base. Certainly in view of the current attitudes of some Hindus towards the Scheduled Castes it would be difficult to say that those values have changed much. In general, therefore, the growth of Buddhism among the low castes, since it embodies an ideology which is in principle destructive of social distinctions, is likely to be viewed with dislike (to say the least) by the majority of those who see themselves primarily as caste Hindus. Thus, the prospects for Buddhism in India, in general terms, are unlikely to have been enhanced by the neo-Buddhist movement among the Mahars and Jatavs.

In his analysis of social disprivilege and conflict in Indian society Ambedkar identified the caste structure as the primary factor responsible. He regarded Buddhism, as an equalitarian social ideology, as the most appropriate (because most thoroughly Indian) replacement. In the hope that this discovery would be made by millions of others, and that its implications would be understood, he envisaged as a not-too-distant possibility the crumbling of the Hindu social order.

In the event what has happened has been the identification of neo-Buddhism with a few disprivileged groups, mainly Mahar and Jatav. Instead of the Buddhist movement resulting in the undermining of the caste system, as he hoped, it has become yet another (low) caste movement. To this, the appropriate response from the majority of Hindus has been in *caste* terms. In other words, a movement which was non-caste or anti-caste in Ambedkar's intention has itself assumed a caste

126

character. Evidently, this cannot be judged to have been a successful policy, given the conditions of modern India.

The Buddhist future in India

Any future Buddhist movement in India, and perhaps elsewhere, will start with the advantage of having before it the lessons of Ambedkarite neo-Buddhism. What others will learn from the course of events in that case and how they will apply them can only be guessed. Whether the future prospects of Buddhism in India will have been adversely affected is also an open question.

If the Ambedkarite type of Buddhism is considered in isolation it would seem that the future of Buddhism in India is to be restricted to a strongly devotional movement in which the cult-hero plays a great part. Of such movements India already has an abundance. Or it might appear as the continuation of a social protest movement which, having tried and failed politically, subsequently turned into a *religious* movement; it might be seen as one of the 're-ligions of the oppressed'.[67] Like Wesleyan Methodism, Ambedka-rite Buddhism will no doubt gradually secure for its followers, through the new ethic which it teaches them, enhanced social and economic prospects as private individuals and thus eventually bring many of them to a fair degree of material prosperity and social respectability.[68] And just as the Rai Das cult among the Camars of Uttar Pradesh described by Cohn enabled those who followed the example of their culture-hero to 'make themselves the equal of anyone',[69] so the Ambedkar cult may function in a similar way as a means of eventual upward social mobility for the Mahar caste. However, this upward mobility of an entire caste *within* the caste system, of which other examples are known,[70] whereby one caste moves up the league table and others, as a result, are necessarily forced down, leaves the overall situation of social and economic disability and discrimination virtually unchallenged and ultimately unchanged.

However, the fact remains that the Buddhism which has resulted from Ambedkar's work is a type of Buddhism, Maharashtrian Buddhism, and must be taken into account in any survey of local cultural patterns of Buddhism; but it cannot be said, at present at any rate, to constitute the new 'all-India' Buddhism which Ambedkar had hoped it would be.

This is a positive, not a negative view of the situation. For the potential for such a new Buddhism certainly exists elsewhere in India. This was mentioned in Chapter 4: the appeal of Buddhism as a philosophy, as a realist understanding of the world, of human nature and of social action. Before Ashoka's time Buddhism was primarily a philosophy of this kind: a system of thought which ruled out animism and its accompanying ritualistic practices, encouraged rational attitudes and criticised the notion of submission to some superhuman power who was supposed to be directing the world-process. During Ashoka's time it acquired a more religious character; there was a marked growth in the veneration of *stupas*, the monuments in which were said to be enshrined the relics of great men and heroes. As I have argued in more detail elsewhere, it was this development, becoming associated with Buddhism, 'which more than anything else marks the beginning of the Buddhist movement in religious terms'.[71] The potential for a modern recovery of Buddhism is probably as great in India as anywhere, especially among the growing but still small section of the people who are aware of a sense of release from tribal and caste restrictions of thought and outlook by education and social reforms. The characteristics of this small but growing minority were noted in Chapter 4,[72] where it was suggested that they fall into two types, the Nehru type and the Ambedkar type. By the latter, it will now be seen, is meant Ambedkar in his early youth, long before the development of the Ambedkar cult and its exclusive identification with one or two Scheduled Castes.

Ambedkar's assertion that every society needs a religion is *not* a self-evident truth. Nor did Ambedkar demonstrate its truth. The same is the case with his contention that what modern Asia needed was a political form of Buddhism. The early Buddhists did not attempt to politicise their movement as, for example, the early Muslims of Arabia did. But they developed a form of organisation, and were probably the first of the philosophical schools to do so. They maintained a distinction between their organisation and the centre of political power, but they also showed that they were not unaware of the importance of the establishment of a just social order and of the role of kings in this connection, *faute de mieux* (for there are indications that they rated a republican system of government more highly than monarchy). For modern Buddhists there is no inherently *Buddhist* necessity for a politicised movement. But there does appear to be good Buddhist reason why they should be concerned with general questions of social order and justice. For Buddhism is a middle way, in social as in other respects. Its social theory from the beginning consisted in the recognition that the most favourable conditions for the practical pursuit of Buddhist aims are to be found in association neither with great affluence and personal power, nor with poverty and deprivation. The Buddhist concern that the optimum conditions for the pursuit of self-understanding should, in the good society, exist for the maximum number of people, has clear implications for social policy.

Ambedkar's insistence on regarding Buddhism, even in a modernised form, as *necessarily* a religion, is also unsupportable. The evidence of the Ambedkarite movement suggests that Buddhism would be more clearly perceived in its essential nature, and would have greater intellectual relevance to citizens of modern India if its non-religious character as a psycho-social philosophy[73] were to be unambiguously set forth. And if in India, most traditionally religious of countries, then everywhere.

Buddhist culture and Buddhist sect

Beyond the very loose characterisation of Buddhism as a 'religion' which Ambedkar used it is possible, on the basis of a review of points raised in this study, to identify two specific *types* of Buddhism or social formations in which Buddhism is an element. It is suggested that these two types, together with any others that may be identified elsewhere, will need to be included in any general typology with which Buddhologists and sociologists of religion may work. Briefly, the two types are: Buddhism as the psycho-social philosophy which has just been mentioned, *with* the particular surrounding culture; and Buddhism in the same sense but *without* cultural embodiment.

Buddhist cultures are many, and the philosophical element is not combined with the culture in any simple or regular way. In each of the many patterns of Buddhist culture, whether Burmese, or Shan, or Thai, or Sinhalese, or any other, there is a social formation which provides the basis for the culture, and in each pattern of Buddhist culture there is a Buddhistic element, each example of which represents the product of the interaction between an original Buddhistic component and the totality of the other, non-Buddhistic elements in the culture. The Buddhistic component in Burmese Buddhist culture, for instance, was received at some relatively distant time in the past, and that component was itself a cultural product of some similar antecedent interaction in Mon culture, or in some South Indian culture, or from wherever it was that the Buddhistic element reached Burmese, or whatever other Buddhist culture. It is therefore very difficult to decide, in any given Buddhist culture, what is Buddhist and what is not. The difficulty is heightened by the fact that no two such cultures are the same. This type of Buddhism, 'Buddhist culture', exists therefore only as an abstraction. It is an abstraction made from a general category. It can be studied only in its actual, empirical examples. For a Buddhist culture is recognisable, if only by the self-definition as 'Buddhists' of those who are its bearers. For the Burmese Buddhist layman, there is no Buddhist 'organisation', membership of which he can quote in support of his claim to be a Buddhist. He performs certain ritual actions and makes certain ritual utterances, but he does so not by virtue of belonging to an organisation, but because these are cultural practices of the people among whom he was born. His attitudes in certain respects to certain occupations, beverages and so on, will distinguish him from the man whose culture is Muslim or Christian or tribal. His *culture* is the only formation which conveys to him his Buddhism. It is not a recognisably religious formation in the sense, for example, in which a church or a sect are. But in the typology of religious formations it cannot be ignored by sociologists of religion as though it were non-existent. True, it is the area of study worked principally by anthropologists. The sociology of religion has in the past, it is true also, tended to be rather culture-bound, restricting itself to Western types of religion. But if it is to be properly comparative in its method, then this type of religious formation has to be included within its range.

The cultural type, in the Buddhist case, appears more complex owing to the fact that within such configurations (Burmese, Shan, Tibetan, etc.) there exists an identifiable organisation, the Sangha, which in certain respects looks very like a church. But the Sangha does not in fact conform with any Western 'church-type'. An important difference is that all its members are full-time professionals. Moreover, except in the case of the monks of Thailand these are organised in discreet, independent local congregations, each presided over by the senior monk in the congregation, although in the Tibetan form there is more of an hierarchical structure. Again, in certain respects the Sangha might be taken to resemble the sect-type. But in this case, the *economic* reliance of the 'sect' members on the lay ('non-sect') people of the surrounding society, a reliance which is religiously sanctioned, is inconsistent with the sect-type generally. Moreover, without the existence of a Sangha in its midst, the formation which has been identified as *Buddhist culture* tends to disintegrate, as we have seen in the case of India in the pre-modern period (Chapter 3). The Sangha is thus, it is clear, an integral element of the autonomous type called Buddhist culture and is not an autonomous type itself.

It is to this type that the Mahar Buddhism of western India and the Jatav Buddhism of Agra may most appropriately be allocated. These two new examples can be added to the list of the various Buddhist cultures of Asia, and each will, no doubt, now develop culturally in its own way.

To characterise Mahar Buddhist culture (or Jadav Buddhist culture) as one more of the sub-cultures of India does not conflict with the earlier characterisation of the new Mahar Buddhism as a cult-hero centred movement, or as a movement with a religious ethic as its core. But for the purposes of exact analysis it may be preferred to call it an *incipient* sub-culture. In the Indian context what is thus incipient will quickly tend to become more recognisably and fully a distinct sub-culture. Certain elements of traditional Mahar culture, together with the memory of Ambedkar as cult-hero, and an ethic put together from Buddhist precepts will, with other local elements, blend to produce the characteristic structure of Mahar Buddhist culture. Already it can be seen taking shape.

Neither of these new Buddhist cultural patterns, however, will have personal relevance for the Nehru type of potential Buddhist, since this type represents a fairly wide range of modern citizens of India for whom traditional caste or tribal or communal identity has ceased to be of importance. For him or her Buddhism is primarily significant in the other sense I have mentioned, that of a psycho-social philosophy *without* cultural embodiment. A parallel which may help to identify this type more clearly is that of a person in the West who is strongly attracted to the philosophy of, let us say, David Hume. Humean philosophy will come to form part of that person's conscious intellectual orientation to life. The fact that he is free to adopt such a stance he owes, in part, to his cultural situation, which has given him (in modern times) the freedom to do so. He owes it also to the fact that he has access to Hume's philosophy (some have not). Another necessary condition is that his own internal, personal configuration is such that he is disposed to respond to it favourably.

The general distinction which I am seeking to make is between Buddhist culture as a received, total cultural pattern, and Buddhism as the philosophical element in a personal way of life. The earliest Buddhists appear to have been of the latter type, whereas the mass of the later Buddhists of India belonged to the type of those who receive Buddhism as a characterising, predominant element of their culture.

The earliest Buddhists were men and women who, freed to some extent from traditional culture and attitudes by the growth in India in the sixth century BC of urban centres and their attendant style of life[74] came upon the teaching of Gautama Buddha, the sage of the Sakya clan, who was one of a number of contemporary propounders of new ways of life and thought which the age had produced. Such men and women, if they were so disposed by their individual natures, circumstances and experiences, responded to the Buddha's philosophy favourably.

It is to their present-day successors, in modern India and elsewhere, that Buddhist philosophy and meditation appeals as relevant and important, and thus becomes perhaps the single most important element in their several stances towards life in an urban, modern context. Such individuals, to whom Buddhism makes primarily this kind of appeal, are before long faced with considerations of a social nature. As soon as an individual of this type begins to acquire an association with other people of the same kind, then, in sociological terms, a *sect* comes into being. And as soon as the members of the sect see their common stance as something which they feel a desire or an obligation to perpetuate, however light this obligation may be, then the nature of the surrounding social order is no longer for them a matter of indifference. In effect this means that they become aware of the surrounding social order in a way in which they were not previously. In some cases the attitude of a sect towards the social order may be negative. That is to say it may be one of conscious non-identification with, or even rejection of the social order. In such cases this will be the full extent of the matter.

In other cases the attitude may be one which recognises a necessity for the replacement of the existing social order by some other. It was in this category, it seems to me, that the early Buddhists belonged. Whether there was an element in the teaching of Gautama which was directly the basis for this attitude, or whether it was an elaboration by the early followers of what they saw to be an implication of Gautama's teaching is not of primary importance compared with the fact that Buddhist Suttas indicate that a certain kind of restructuring of the social order was in early Buddhism regarded as desirable. Possibly in this category with the early Buddhists belong their latter-day successors in modern societies. Certainly it is more likely to be within the sect-type that this attitude will be found. There can, however, be no certainty on that point, nor on any other, for nothing can with certainty be predicted of sects.

I have characterised the Buddhism of the modern sect type in terms of philosophy and meditation. This, too, is as precise a characterisation as it is possible to offer. One has necessarily to employ these terms in an impressionistic sense. 'Philosophical' in this context refers to the initially intellectual appeal which Buddhist teaching makes to those who find themselves out of sympathy with the 'blind faith' or the escapist character of other modes of individual orientation. But on the other hand, there soon comes an appreciation of the fact that Buddhism in modern society is not a purely intellectual affair in the sense of allowing one to remain a mere spectator. In the first instance Buddhist teaching may be expressed as a reasoned analysis in terms of human experience, but it is soon seen to have the clear implication of some kind of practice.

Thus, an adequate account of the constituency in which potential Buddhists of the sect type will be found would have to include institutions such as the Maha Bodhi Society, or the group of intellectuals at Banaras called the Indian Humanist Society, described briefly by Fiske,[75] and an institution such as the Vipassana International Academy at Dhammagiri near Bombay. The last of these, connected with the famous Burmese meditation teacher U Ba Khin, offers ten-day courses of meditational practice which regularly attract about two hundred participants, the majority of whom are Indian and predominantly middle class.[76]

The known examples of Buddhism in India today thus fall into one or other of the two types which have just been characterised. First, there are the patterns of *Buddhist culture*, which include those of Tibetan or Burmese or Shan origin in the north-east, and of Tibetan origin in the north-west. There are also pockets of refugee Tibetan culture in a few places elsewhere, mainly near Mysore. And there are the new, developing Buddhist cultures of Maharashtra and Agra.

Second, there is the *sect* type, which is still rare. This, of course, is not its own name for itself, but simply a sociologist's category.[77] Where examples of it are found in India today they are likely to be called 'Societies'.[78] The emerging class of younger people who have undergone higher education and have consciously stepped out of their tribal or caste cultural environment, and who may declare themselves to be sceptics or secularists and not interested in religion, in the sense of belief in some supernatural power, can be expected, if they acquire an interest in Buddhistic philosophy and practice, to turn towards groups such as these.

It may seem that there has been little substantial revival of Buddhism in India since Mrs Rhys Davids contemplated the possibility seventy years ago. There has, nevertheless, been a quickening of interest, and the potential for renewal still exists. This is not the place for predictions, but he would be a bold (and possibly rash) man who said that either, or both, of the two types which have been identified here would not, in another seventy years, have proved to be agencies of much more substantial Buddhist revival in India.

Notes

CHAPTER 1

1. Shwe Zan Aung, *Compendium of Philosophy*, edited by C. Rhys Davids (1910) p. xv.
2. T. W. Rhys Davids, *Buddhist India* (1903; repr. 1970) p. v.
3. Ibid.
4. Ibid.
5. On the terminology used in connection with these groups, see p. 67.
6. See p. 91.
7. The *Bahishkrit Hitakatini Sabha*; see p. 79.
8. See Keer, (1962), Kuber (1973) and Lokhande (1977).
9. See Fiske (1972), Lynch (1969) and Zelliott (1966).

CHAPTER 2

1. See K. P. Chattopadhyaya in *Journal of the Royal Asiatic Society of Bengal*, vol. VIII (1942) pp. 131–3.
2. See E. Fischoff's preface to his translation of Max Weber's *The Sociology of Religion* (1963) p. x.
3. See Max Weber, *The Sociology of Religion* (1963) pp. 266f.
4. Cf. Trevor Ling, *A History of Religion East and West* (1968) pp. 135ff.
5. See Mendelson, E.M., *Sangha and State in Burma* (1976).
6. See T. Ling, *Buddhism and the Mythology of Evil* (1962) pp. 12ff. The same phenomenon was already to be found fully developed in the Pali texts, and we now have a most useful exposition of the full extent of the relevant material in Dr Marasinghe's *Gods in Early Buddhism*. So far as the continuing, contemporary existence of this fertile relationship is concerned there is the excellent analysis provided by S. J. Tambiah's *Buddhism and the Spirit Cults in North-East Thailand* (1970).

CHAPTER 3

1. R. C. Mitra, 'The decline of Buddhism in India', *Visva-Bharati Annals*, vol. VI (1954) pp. 161–4.
2. S. Radhakrishnan, *Indian Philosophy*, vol. I, p. 609.

3. C. Eliot, *Hinduism and Buddhism*, vol. II (1921) p. 108.
4. Op cit., p. 127.
6. Ibid.
7. This view has been challenged most recently by Lalmoni Joshi in his *Studies in the Buddhistic Culture of India* (1967) pp. 324–9.
8. E. Durkheim, *Elementary Forms of the Religious Life* (1961) p. 356.
9. B. C. Law, *Indological Studies*, vol. III (1954) p. 62.
10. Bongard-Levin, 'Epigraphic document of the Mauryas from Bengal', *Journal of the Asiatic Society of Bengal*, vol. XXIV (1958) p. 83.
11. B. M. Morrison, *Political Centres and Culture Regions in Early Bengal* (1970) pp. 13f.
12. W. W. Hunter, *Annals of Rural Bengal* (1897) p. 99.
13. *The Travels of Fa-Hsien (399–414 AD) or, Record of the Buddhistic Kingdoms*, retranslated Giles (1927) pp. 65f.
14. S. K. Maity and R. R. Mukherjee, *Corpus of Bengal Inscriptions*, no. 10 (1967) p. 68.
15. Joshi, op. cit., p. 318.
16. Ibid., p. 326.
17. S. Beal, *Buddhistic Records of the Western World*, vol. II (1884) p. 194. Pundra Vardhana corresponds roughly to the modern districts of Dinajpur, Bogra, Rajshai, Pabna, Mymensingh and Dacca, in Bangladesh.
18. Beal, op. cit., pp. 200f.
19. Ibid., p. 202.
20. S. Hussain, *Everyday Life in the Pala Empire*, Asiatic Society of Pakistan, publication no. 23, (1968) pp. 23ff.
21. Ibid., p. 45.
22. Loc. cit.
23. A. M. Chowdhury, *Dynastic History of Bengal, 750–1200 AD*, Asiatic Society of Pakistan, publication no. 21 (1967) p. 182.
24. Morrison, op. cit., p. 154.
25. Preface to *Taranatha's History of Buddhism in India*, trsl. by Lama Chimpa and Alaka Chattopadhyaya (Simla, 1970) p. xi.
26. Ibid., pp. xii–xiii.
27. R. C. Majumdar, *History of Ancient Bengal* (1971) pp. 526–7.
28. Cf. Majundar, op. cit., p. 524: 'The establishment of the Buddhist Pála dynasty in Bengal was probably facilitated by the growing dominance of Buddhism in this region.'
29. See T. O. Ling, *The Buddha* (1973) pp. 117–19 and 67ff.
30. See T. O . Ling, *Buddhism and the Mythology of Evil* (1962) pp. 11–21.
31. See T. O. Ling, *The Buddha* (1973) pp. 120ff.
32. Morrison, op. cit., p. 16.
33. S. K. Chatterji, *The Origin and Development of the Bengali Language*, vol. I (1926) p. 80.
34. D. Snellgrove and H. Richardson, *A Cultural History of Tibet* (1968) p. 129.
35. Joshi, op. cit., pp. 394–401.
36. Maity, op. cit. (note 14) p. 96.
37. As, for instance, by R. C. Mitra, in *Visvabharati Annals*, vol. VI (1954) pp. 126–8.

NOTES

38. Such as R. C. Mitra, in loc. cit.
39. *Indian Philosophy*, vol. 1, p. 609.
40. Ibn Battuta: *Travels in Asia and Africa, 1325–1354*, trans. and selected by H. A. R. Gibb (London, 1929) pp. 96.
41. Nihar Ranjan Ray himself suggested this to me in a personal conversation in Calcutta in February 1974. See also S. Dutt, *Buddhism in East Asia*, p. 74.
42. Ling, op. cit. (1973) pp. 202f.
43. Ibid., pp. 206f.

CHAPTER 4

1. Exact figure given: 3,812,325. (*Census of India, 1971. Series I, India, Paper 2: Religion.*)
2. The largest concentrations outside the north-east and the north-west were in Uttar Pradesh (39,500), mostly in Meerut and Agra Districts; and Delhi (9000). The only other states with more than even 3000 were Mysore (14,000), Orissa (8500), Gujerat (5500), Bihar (5000) and Rajasthan (3500). Figures given are correct to the nearest 500.
3. Eleanor Zelliott, 'Buddhism and politics in Maharashtra', in *South Asian Politics and Religion*, ed. by D. E. Smith (1966) p. 191n1.
4. Figures (correct to the nearest 500) are as follows: the north-eastern area 101,000; the north-western area 38,500; the rest of India 17,500. (Sources: *Census of India 1931*, vol. I, *India*, Part II, by J. H. Hutton (Delhi, 1933) p. 517, and vol V Part II, by A. E. Porter, (Calcutta, 1932) tables, p. 221.
5. *Manchester Guardian*, 18 October 1956.
6. Balkrishna Govind Gikhale, *Buddhism in Maharashtra: A History* (Bombay, 1976) p. 158.
7. *Census of India 1931, vol. I, India*, Part I, *Report*, by J. H. Hutton (Delhi, 1933) p. 389.
8. Gokhale, op. cit., pp. 158f.
9. *Bengal District Gazetteers: Darjeeling*, by L. S. S. O'Malley (Calcutta, 1907), p. 35.
10. J. D. Hooker, *Himalaya Journals* vol. 1 (1854) p. 127.
11. E. T. Dalton, *Descriptive Ethnology of Bengal* (Calcutta, 1872) p. 101.
12. J. A. H. Louis, *The Gates of Thibet* (1895) pp. 95 and 112.
13. J. Claude White, *Sikkim and Bhutan* (1909; repr. 1971) pp. 7 and 14.
14. C. von Fürer-Haimendorf, *The Sherpas of Nepal* (London 1964) p. 1.
15. Nirmala Das, *The Dragon Country: the General History of Bhutan* (1974) p. 5.
16. D. L. Snellgrove, *Buddhist Himalaya* (1957) pp. 212f.
17. C. J. Morris, et al., *Nepal and the Gurkhas* (London, 1965) p. 112.
18. Alexander W. Macdonald, 'The Tamang as seen by one of themselves' in *Essays on the Ethnology of Nepal and South Asia* (Kathmandu, 1975) pp. 132–3.
19. Information from an interview with Sri Gising Tamang in Darjeeling, 14 April 1976.
20. Sangharakshita, *The Thousand Petalled Lotus* (London, 1976) pp. 270–84.
21. By calculation from Census of India Reports for 1931, 1951 and 1971.
22. See, e.g. K. K. Siddh, *Family Planning: the Religious Factor* (New Delhi, 1974).

137

On Buddhist population growth see: T. Ling, 'Buddhist factors in population growth and control: a survey based on Thailand and Ceylon', in *Population Studies*, vol. 23, Part I, March 1969.
23. *Imperial Gazetteer of India* by W. W. Hunter, vol. I (1881) p. 247.
24. B. K. Roy-Burman, 'Modernization among tribal people on India's borders', in *Studies in Social Change*, ed. by K. S. Mathur *et al.* (Lucknow, 1973) p. 109.
25. Verrier Elwin, *A Philosophy for N.E.F.A.* (Shillong, 1959) p. 216.
26. Roy-Burman, op. cit., pp. 125f.
27. Ibid, p. 127.
28. See Trevor Ling, *The Buddha: Buddhist Civilisation in India and Ceylon* (London, 1973) Part 2.
29. Elwin, op. cit., p. 219.
30. Ibid., p. 211.
31. Sangharakshita, op. cit., p. 121.
32. D. E. Smith, *Religion and Politics in Burma* (Princeton, New Jersey, 1965) p. 251.
33. Heinz Bechert, 'Theravada Buddhist Sangha: some general observations on historical and political factors in its development' in *Journal of Asian Studies* vol. 29, no. 4 (1970) pp. 770, 772 and 778.
34. Fiske (1976) pp. 135f.

CHAPTER 5

1. The term is used by Harold R. Isaacs, for example—see *The Untouchables*, ed. J. Michael Mahar (1972) ch. 13.
2. 'Pollution and poverty', in Mahar, op. cit., p. 413.
3. Ibid., p 420.
4. Dhananjay Keer, *Dr Ambedkar: Life and Mission*, 2nd edn (1962) pp. 1f.
5. Keer, op. cit., p.2.
6. J. A. Dubois, *Hindu Manners, Customs, and Ceremonies*, trsl. by Henry K. Beauchamp, 3rd edn. (1906; repr. 1968) p. 49.
7. Op. cit., p. 50.
8. Op. cit., p. 50f.
9. Op. cit., pp. 110f.
10. Op. cit., p. 49.
11. Mahar (1972) p. xi.
12. Béteille, in Mahar (1972) pp. 416f.
13. Op. cit. (1961) pp. 234ff.
14. M. K. Pande (ed.), *Social Life in Rural India* (Calcutta, 1977) pp. 1–87.
15. See, for example, the state-by-state analysis of atrocities on Harijans between 1974 and 1977 in the *Statesman* newspaper (Calcutta), 3 October 1978, and the leading article, *Statesman*, 4 October 1978.
16. B. G. Ghokale (1976) p. 16.
17. Ibid.
18. Keer, op. cit., p. 13.
19. Ibid.
20. Keer, op. cit., p. 19.

21. Keer, op. cit., p. 21.
22. Keer, op. cit., p. 27.
23. Keer, op. cit., p. 168.
24. Bernard S. Cohn, 'Changing traditions of a low caste', in *Traditional India*, ed. by Milton Singer (1959) p. 215.
25. Ibid.
26. Op. cit., p. 214.
27. Ibid.
28. Op. cit., p. 215.
29. M. M. Thomas, *The Secular Ideologies of India and the Secular Meaning of Christ* (1975) p. 124.
30. B. C. Allen, *East Bengal District Gazetteers: Dacca*, (1912) p. 68.
31. L. S. S. O'Malley *East Bengal District Gazetteers: Jessore.*
32. J. H. Broomfield, *Elite Conflict in a Plural Society* (1968), p. 158.
33. Quoted in Broomfield, op. cit., p. 273.
34. Under the terms of the Government of India Act 1935.
35. Broomfield, op. cit., p. 310.
36. Op. cit., pp. 312f.
37. Thomas, op. cit., p. 126.
38. Ibid.
39. Ibid.
40. Thomas, op. cit., p. 125.
41. Op. cit., p. 129.
42. Keer, op. cit., p. 56.
43. Ambedkar, op. cit. (1945) pp. 251–4.
44. Keer, op. cit., p. 59.
45. Keer, op. cit., p. 62.
46. Keer, op. cit., pp. 100f.
47. W. N. Kuber, *Dr Ambedkar: A Critical Study* (1973) p. 56.
48. Keer, op. cit., p. 251.
49. Keer, op. cit., pp. 252f.
50. Keer, op. cit., p. 268.
51. Ambedkar, *The Annihilation of Caste* (1936) p. 49.
52. Keer, op. cit., p. 302.
53. Kuber, op. cit., p. 58.
54. Keer, op. cit., pp. 488, 495, 517.
55. Keer, op. cit., p. 517.
56. Kuber, op. cit., p. 306.

CHAPTER 6

1. Selig Harrison, *India: the most Dangerous Decades* (1960) p. 109.
2. Sankar Ghose, *Socialism and Communism in India* (1971) p. 310.
3. Keer, op. cit., p. 61.
4. Ibid., p. 299.
5. Ibid., pp. 298f.
6. Ibid., p. 435.
7. Ibid., p. 444.

8. Ibid., p. 258.
9. B. R. Ambedkar, 'The Buddha and the Future of His Religion', *Maha Bodhi* (April–May 1950) pp. 202f.
10. See B. R. Ambedkar, *Pakistan*, pp. 215–38.
11. Ibid.
12. T. S. Wilkinson and M. M. Thomas, *Ambedkar and the Neo-Buddhist Movement* (1972) pp. 59–61.
13. Keer, p. 283.
14. Ibid., p. 272.
15. Ibid., p. 273 (emphasis added).
16. See Trevor Ling, *Karl Marx and Religion* (Macmillan, London forthcoming).
17. He ended his speech with a quotation from the last words of the Buddha, a quotation which could be, and was, taken as an indication of his intention. Keer, op. cit., p. 274. According to D. C. Ahir, *Buddhism and Ambedkar* (New Delhi, 1968) p. 29, the quotation used was, 'Be lamps unto yourselves' (*Maha parinibbana Sutta*).
18. Mark Galanter, 'Untouchability and the Law' in *The Untouchables in Contemporary India*, ed. by J. Michael Mahar (1972) p. 241.
19. Keer, op. cit., p. 418.
20. Keer, p. 419.
21. Keer, p. 420.
22. Ibid.
23. Keer, p. 495.
24. Ibid.
25. Keer, p. 503 (emphasis added).
26. Keer, p. 487 (emphasis added).
27. Keer, p. 504.
28. Keer, p. 505.
29. *Maha Bodhi* (Dec. 1959); *Light of the Dhamma* (Jan. 1959). See Keer, p. 518.
30. D. C. Ahir, *Buddhism and Ambedkar* (1968) pp. 9f. and 32.
31. Keer, op. cit., p. 516.
32. The contrast between the two is a theme which frequently occurs in the writing of British administrators. The following passage is an example:

A Hindu gentleman, orthodox but emancipated, after a tour in Burma, did me the honour of dining at my table. In the course of the evening he said to me that, after seeing Burma, he thought it much to be regretted that Buddhism had not maintained itself as the prevailing religion of India.

Thus wrote Sir Henry Thirkell White, a British administrator in Burma, in the latter part of the nineteenth century.

CHAPTER 7

1. N. R. Chakravarti, *The Indian Minority in Burma* (1971) p. 89.
2. Ibid., p. 91.
3. The foregoing two paragraphs are reproduced, with some alterations, from my paper 'Max Weber in India', *Leeds University Review*, vol. 16, no. 1 (May 1973) pp. 59–61.

NOTES

4. See Raymond Owens 'Mahisya Entrepreneurs in Howrah, West Bengal' in *Bengal: Change and Continuity*, ed. by R. and M. J Beech (Michigan, 1970).
5. See H. N. C. Stevenson, *The Economics of the Central Chin Tribes* (1943).
6. In this connection, particularly *The Religion of India* (trsl. 1958), and *The Sociology of Religion* (trsl. 1963).
7. *The Sociology of Religion*, p. 268f.
8. Op. cit., p. 267.
9. *The Religion of India*, p. 255.
10. Ibid., pp. 116f.
11. *The Sociology of Religion*, p. 83.
12. Ibid., p. 268.
13. Ibid., pp. 61f.
14. Ibid., p. 62.
15. *The Sociology of Religion*, p. 210.
16. Ibid., p. 247.
17. Ibid., p. 42.
18. P. Bigandet, *The Life or Legend of Gautama, the Buddha of the Burmese*, 2nd edn. (Rangoon, 1866).
19. *The Soul of a People* (1903) p. 130.
20. Ibid., p. 130.
21. Ibid., p. 136.
22. Shway Yoe, *The Burman: his Life and Notions*, p. 124.
23. D. Pfanner and J. Ingersoll, 'Theravada Buddhism and Village Economic Behaviour,' *Journal of Asian Studies*, vol XXI, no. 3 (May 1962) p. 342.
24. Ibid.
25. Op. cit., p. 361.
26. Hurst (London, 1977).
27. Pfanner and Ingersoll, op. cit., p. 361 (emphasis added).
28. Ibid., p. 349.
29. Ibid., p. 348.
30. Ibid., p. 343.
31. See above p. 97.
32. *The Soul of a People*, p. 117.
33. Pfanner, op. cit., p. 344.
34. Ibid., p. 345.
35. Ibid., p. 348.
36. Ibid., p. 349.
37. Ibid., p. 360.
38. Manning Nash, *The Golden Road to Modernity*, 1965.
39. Nash, op. cit., p. 156.
40. Nash, op. cit., p. 162.
41. Op. cit., p. 156.
42. Pali, *Kusala*, that which is of wholesome moral effect.
43. Nash, op. cit., p. 161.
44. Melford Spiro, 'Buddhism and Economic Action in Burma', in *American Anthropologist*, vol. 68, no. 5 (Oct. 1966).
45. Spiro, op. cit., p. 1166.

CHAPTER 8

1. *Census of India, 1971*, Series 1, Paper 2, 1972, *Religion*, p. 22.
2. The nearest is Akola District, which had 16·15 per cent in 1971. Source, ibid.

3. *Census of India, 1971,* Series 1, Pt. II-A(ii) *Union Primary Census Abstract* (Delhi, 1974).
4. See Adele Fiske (1972) pp. 122 and 124.
5. J. S. Wilkinson (1972) p. 97.
6. Fiske (1970) pp. 142f.
7. Fiske (1972) p. 135.
8. Ibid., p. 136.
9. Ibid.
10. See p. 62.
11. See p. 91.
12. B. Ambedkar, *The Buddha and His Dhamma* (1957) pp. 425–35.
13. Ambedkar, op. cit., p. 434.
14. Op. cit., p. 435.
15. M. Spiro, *Buddhism and Society* (1971); pp. 284–6, 'The Function of Monasticism'.
16. Ambedkar, op. cit., p. 103.
17. Op. cit., p. 104.
18. Op. cit., p. 513. See also pp. 337–44.
19. Briefly, the doctrine that every pheonomenon, whether physical and mental, is conditioned by antecedent factors upon which it is dependent, the whole forming an uninterrupted flux. See Trevor Ling, *The Buddha* (Penguin Books, 1976) pp. 132ff.
20. Nyanatiloka, *Buddhist Dictionary* (Colombo, 1956) p. 73.
21. *Visuddhimagga,* XIX. It is important to notice, also, however, that the annihilation of all the factors, material and mental, which have constituted an individual, is also rejected by Buddhist orthodoxy. No human life is without its subsequent 'reverberations' in some other form of life, human or non-human, but this is not the rebirth of the same individual 'soul'.
22. Ambedkar, op. cit., p. 91.
23. *Social Life in Rural India,* ed. by M. K. Pandhe; sponsored by the Academy of Political and Social Studies (Poona, 1977) p. 96.
24. G. C. Mandal *et. al., The Economy of Rural Change: a Study of Eastern India* (1974) pp. 71–3.
25. Wilkinson (1972) p. 95.
26. Op. cit., p. 98.
27. Ibid.
28. Op. cit., p. 99.
29. M. Glen and Sipra Bose Johnson, in *Cohesion and Conflict in Modern India,* ed. Giri Raj Gupta (1978) p. 91.
30. Isaacs (1972) p. 377.
31. Fiske (1970) p. 142.
32. Zelliott (1966) pp. 205f.
33. Lokhande (1977) p. 250.
34. Max Weber, *The Sociology of Religion,* trsl. by Ephraim Fischoff (1963) p. 55.
35. See Lynch (1969 and 1972).
36. Lynch (1969) p. 130; see also Lynch (1972) p. 106.
37. Lynch (1972) p. 107.
38. Reported by the Agra daily newspaper *Sainik,* 20 March 1956. See Lynch (1969) p. 138; and (1972) p. 107f.
39. Lynch (1972) p. 109.
40. Ibid., p. 110.
41. Ibid., p. 111. See E. R. Leach, *Political Systems of Highland Burma* (1965) pp. 264–8.
42. Zelliott (1966) p. 200.

43. Zelliott (1972) p. 91.
44. Zelliott (1966) p. 204.
45. See p. 91.
46. Zelliott (1966) p. 207.
47. Ibid., p. 204.
48. Lokhande (1977) ch. 2.
49. Ibid., pp. 24f.
50. J. Michal Mahar, 'Agents of Dharma' in Mahar (1972) p. 35.
51. Zelliott (1972) p. 94.
52. Fiske (1972) p. 122.
53. Zelliott (1966) pp. 207f.
54. Ibid., p. 209.
55. Lynch (1969) p. 106.
56. Kuber (1973) p. 293.
57. See contributions by Mahapatra, Sinha, Ekka, Sen and Vidyarthi in K. Suresh Singh (ed.), *Tribal Situation in India* (Indian Institute of Advanced Study, 1972) pp. 399–453.
58. Lynch (1969) p. 102. Dushkin (1972) p. 200.
59. Dushkin, L., in Mahar (1972) p. 201.
60. Santokh Singh Anant, 'Caste Hindu Attitudes: the Harijans' Perception', in *Asian Survey*, vol XI, no. 3 (March 1971) p. 278.
61. Betaille (1972) pp. 419f.
62. B. N. Juyal, 'The Politics of Untouchability in Uttar Pradesh', in *Religion and Society*, vol. XXI, no. 3 (Sept. 1974) pp. 62–81.
63. Ibid., p. 78.
64. Ibid., p. 77.
65. Ibid., p. 81.
66. P. Sivanandan, 'Economic Backwardness of Harijans in Kerala', in *Social Scientist*, vol. 4, no. 10 (May 1976) p. 26.
67. See Vittorio Lanternari, *Religions of the Oppressed* (1963).
68. Trevor Ling, *A History of Religion East and West* (1968) pp. 322f.
69. See Chapter 5, pp. 73f.
70. See, e.g., James Silverberg (ed), *Social Mobility in the Caste System in India* (Comparative Studies in Society and History, Supplement III, 1968).
71. See Trevor Ling, *The Buddha: Buddhist Civilisation in India and Ceylon* (Penguin Books, 1976) p. 202. See also pp. 16–25 and 142–8.
72. See Chapter 4, pp. 58ff.
73. Ling (1976) pp. 142ff (see note 71).
74. Ibid., pp. 51–7.
75. Fiske (1976) p. 135.
76. One indication of their middle class social location is that the majority of those who take the courses are observed to arrive in motor cars. In India this is more clearly a sign of middle class affluence than in the West.
77. Strictly this is not a sociological, but a theological and ecclesiastical category which sociologists have used.
78. Such, e.g., as The Maha Bodhi Society.

Bibliographical References

Ambedkar and neo-Buddhism

Ahir, D. C. *Buddhism and Ambedkar* (New Delhi, 1968).
Ambedkar, B. R. *The Evolution of Provincial Finance in British India* (London, 1925).
——, *The Annihilation of Caste* (Bombay, 1936).
——, *What Congress and Gandhi have done to the Untouchables* (Bombay, 1945).
——, *Pakistan or Partition of India* (Bombay, 1946).
——, *The Untouchables* (New Delhi, 1948).
——, 'The Buddha and the Future of His Religion', in *Maha-Bodhi* (April–May, 1950).
——, *The Buddha and His Dhamma* (Bombay, 1957).
Bétaille, A. 'Pollution and Poverty', in Mahar (1972).
Fiske, Adele 'Religion and Buddhism Among India's New Buddhists', *Social Research*, vol. 36 (1969).
——, 'The Understanding of "Religion" and "Buddhism" among India's New Buddhists', in Wilkinson (1972).
——, 'Scheduled Caste Buddhist Organisations', in Mahar (1972).
——, 'Buddhism in India Today', in *Buddhism in the Modern World*, ed. Heinrich Dumoulin (New York and London, 1976).
Gokhale, B. G. 'Dr Bimrao Ramji Ambedkar: Rebel Against Hindu Tradition', in *Religion and Social Conflict in South Asia*, ed. by Bardwell Smith (1976).
Isaacs, H. R. 'The Ex-Untouchables', in Mahar (1972).
Keer, Dhananjay *Dr. Ambedkar: Life and Mission*, 2nd edn (Bombay, 1962).
Kuber, W. N. *Dr Ambedkar: a Critical Study* (New Delhi, 1973).
Lokhande, G. S. *Bhimrao Ramji Ambedkar: a Study in Social Democracy* (New Delhi, 1977).
Lynch, Owen M. *The Politics of Untouchability: Social Mobility and*

Social Change in a City of India (New York, 1969).
——, 'Dr B. R. Ambedkar – Myth and Charisma', in Mahar (1972).
Mahar, J. Michael (ed.), *The Untouchables in Contemporary India* (Tucson, Arizona, 1972).
Wilkinson, T. S. and Thomas, M. M. (eds), *Ambedkar and the Neo-Buddhist Movement* (Madras, 1972).
Zelliott, Eleanor 'Buddhism and Politics in Maharashtra', in *South Asian Politics and Religion*, ed. by Donald Eugene Smith (Princeton, 1966).
——, 'Gandhi and Ambedkar – a Study in Leadership', in Mahar (1972).

Index

INDEX

Mendelson, E.M., 17, 135
Mhow, 71
Mitra, R.C., 135, 137
Mizoram, 57, 59
Montague-Chelmsford reforms, 75
Morris, C.J., 137
Morrison, B.M., 29, 34, 38, 136
Moscow, 85
Mukherjee, R.R., 136
Murmis, 53
Muslim invaders, 40, 42, 46, 89
Muslims, Darjeeling District, 56
  East Bengal, 75f
  Indian, 86, 123
Mysore, 10, 134

Nagpur, 121
Namasudras, 67, 74
Nash, Manning, 104f, 141
Navayana, 91
Nazimuddin, Sir K., 76
Ne Win, 93
Nehru, Jawaharlal, 49, 58, 82, 88, 128
Neo-Buddhism, 91, 107f, 110, 113f, 116, 118, 122, 126f
Neo-Buddhists, 4, 5, 48, 114, 116, 123, 126
Nepal, 52, 54f, 57
Nepalese language, 53
Nepalis, 53, 57
New York Columbia University, 12, 117
Newars, 53
Nonconformists, 5
North Bengal, 51
North Cachar Hills, 57
Nu, U, 92
Nyanatiloka, 142

O'Malley, L.S.S., 139
Outcastes, 67
Owens, Raymond, 141

Padma Sambhava, 52
Pakistan, Muslims of, 5
  East, 76
Pala kings, 33–8, 46
Pali language and canon, 17, 18, 29

Pande, M.K., 70, 138, 142
Pariahs, 67ff
Parsi community, 94
Paticca-samuppada, 112
Pfanner, D., 100–4, 141
Phule, Jotirao, 76ff
Political Buddhism, 91, 122
Popular beliefs and practices, Buddhist attitude to, 37
Pradhan, as surname, 54
Prajna-paramita, 35
Prophet, exemplary/ethical, 116, 119
'Protestant', as analytical term, 17
Protestant Ethic, 96, 104f

Radhakrishnan, S., 41, 136
Rai, Das, 74, 127
Rajagriha, 18
Ramaswamy, E.V., 77f
Ramraj, 8
Rangoon, 90f, 93
Ray, Nihar Ranjan, 137
Rebirth, doctrine of, 112f
Religion, Ambedkar's view of, 86, 88
Religionssoziologie, 16
Republican Party, 81, 120ff
Rhys Davids, C., 3, 4, 134
  T.W., 3, 135
Richardson, H., 136
Round Table Conferences, 79, 118
Roy-Burman, B.K., 61, 138
Russian Communism, 84, 91

Saiva cults, 89
Sakyamuui, 60
Sangha, 18, 19, 26
Sangharakshita, 54, 62, 110, 137, 138
Santals, 43
Sarnath, 122
Sasanka, 40
Sastri, Hariprasad, 12
Scheduled Caste Federation, 82, 120
Scheduled Castes, 4, 63, 67ff, 70, 73, 76, 90, 107, 109, 117, 122, 124f, 128
  Tribes, 59, 120, 122f
Scott, Sir J.G., 99
Second World War, 88, 93

150